Testimonies Gained and Lessons Learned

Along My Journey of Faith

Gina Gholston

ALONG THE JOURNEY

Any emphasis added to Scripture quotations is the author's own.

Printed in the United States of America

ISBN: 9798287200664

Edit/Layout by Jim Bryson (JamesLBryson@gmail.com)

Cover design by David Munoz (davidmunoznvtn@gmail.com)

Cover photo taken by Gina Gholston

Author photo on back cover courtesy of the media ministry at Church Alive International Roanoke, Virginia

Contents

Dedication

One of the greatest blessings in my life is my family. Growing up, my parents, grandparents, aunts, and uncles were always great role models and encouragers for me. My spiritual heritage runs deep, and my life has been greatly impacted by those roots. My story would be completely different without their influence.

My aunt, Martha (Mot) Holland Pittman, is the one who strongly encouraged me to write this book. She loved to hear me tell the stories of how God has worked in and through my life. She would so often say, "You need to write those stories in a book so others will know that the Lord is real." Her greatest desire was that her family and all others would know God and Jesus.

She has now moved to Heaven, and though she won't be able to read this book, which is actually the result of her encouragement, I know she would be so happy to know that I have written it. So, it is in her honor and memory that I dedicate it.

1

The Knowing Is in the Going

Thus says the Lord, "Stand by the roads and look; ask for the ancient paths, where the good way is, then walk in it, and you will find rest for your souls."

–Jeremiah 6:16 AMP

"There could be fog on the mountain, so you be careful!" These were the instructions from my mom as I was preparing to leave her house one morning. Years of experience had taught her that driving across that mountain could be a bit tricky when the thick fog was settled in. However, from our view in the valley, it was hard to tell if the top of the mountain was still foggy, so she continued by saying, "Sometimes at this time of day, the fog has already lifted, but that's not always certain. You just won't know until you get there."

Life is a journey that we are all on. Between birth and death lies the journey. It's the time we are allotted on this earth, our time on the timeline of God's plan. Our time here is not a dress rehearsal. When all is said and done, we won't get a "do-over." This is it. This is our time, and that time is shrinking with every passing day.

God has created each one of us with purpose, and yet He also created us with the ability to choose what we will do with the life and the time we have been given. Some will choose to allow the uncertainties to keep them from living in the fullness of God's intentions. They misinterpret the fog ahead and allow assumptions to persuade them that taking the journey is just too big a risk, so they become content with containment which seems a safer alternative. It has been said, "A ship in harbor is safe, but that is not what ships are built for."[1] The familiar place may seem safe and certain, but we were not made for containment in the familiar place. The appeal of the comfortable, less challenging path may seem inviting, but the end result of that choice will be a life that is lived with unrealized potential, purpose, and possibility.

Strewn along our journey are many undiscovered adventures and even some uncertainties. We won't always know what may lie ahead. The knowing is only found in the going. That's the purpose of faith in God. Faith doesn't require certainties, for we do not look at the things which are seen, but to the things which are not seen (see 2 Corinthians 4:18). Faith in God requires focus and trust—focus on Him and trust in His promise and ability to lead and guide us every step of the way.

We all have a part in God's plan. He has charted the course for each of our lives, and the journey is ours for the taking. Our choice to focus on and follow Him is not based on an assumption that we understand everything; it is based on our faith in Him. That faith gives us courage to look beyond ourselves and trust the One who is ordering our steps. By faith, we can run the race that has been set before us. We may not fully understand every step we must take–and there may be times when we are not even really convinced that we should follow what we feel to be God's leading–but courageous faith in Him enables us to abandon distracting emotions and go anyway. He is calling each of us to follow Him. He is a trustworthy and able guide, and when we are convinced of that, His voice becomes louder than our human reasoning. Then we are provoked to take those steps that will allow us to accumulate experiences with the Lord that we would have never discovered in the safe and familiar place.

The way forward may seem to have obstacles, and the fog of uncertainty may seem to loom in the distance, but still, we must press on. The obstacles and uncertainties will only make the journey all the more interesting and the testimonies all the more powerful when we come out on the other side!

The One who sees the way–the One who is the Way, Jesus–has gone before us, and His invitation to us all is, "Come! Follow Me!"

The Journey Beckons

The allure of the journey God had charted for my life began to beckon me, even as a young girl. Though I didn't fully understand it all and I haven't made all the right choices, still there has always been a deep knowing that my life belongs to Him. I somehow knew that if I would trust Him, He would lead me and He would work for me, in me, and through me to make Himself known to me and to those around me. The deep in Him calls to the deep inside me, and His bidding voice draws me to keep following those paths that lead me to continually discover Him and the fullness of His purposes for my life.

I have chosen to follow Christ, and the journey so far has been amazing! Along the way, I have experienced God's provision, His healing, His presence, His love, correction, forgiveness, long-suffering, grace, mercy, protection, and guidance. I have received His supernatural wisdom and instruction, and I have witnessed His wonder-working power demonstrated in signs, wonders, and miracles. I am awed by Him! The longer I walk with Him, the more I experience Him, and the more I experience Him, the easier it is to trust His leading. I still do not always understand the leading, and the journey certainly is not always easy, but I have learned that if I keep following Him, He will always prove Himself to be faithful, and my obedience to Him will always lead me to the revealing of His purposes!

Within the pages of this book, I will share a few stories from my journey so far. These stories are not in chronological order, but just randomly recalled and shared. It is not my intention for this book to be autobiographical, but more of a collection of testimonies of some of my personal encounters and experiences with the Lord and lessons I've learned as I've taken this journey of faith. I have also included some stories of things I have witnessed that God has done in others.

There are many experiences and details that I could include in the pages of a book. As a minister, I have witnessed God move in powerful ways in meetings to save the lost, heal the sick, and deliver those who were bound by addictions, oppression, depression, and other mental and spiritual strongholds. However, I didn't want to make this book just about what I've seen and experienced in meetings. I wanted it to be more about personal experiences—how I've seen God move in powerful ways, even in my everyday life. These testimonies reveal His goodness and the reality of His love and involvement in our lives as we live and choose to walk with Him.

My stories are personal, but they are not exclusive. There are numerous people with volumes and volumes of testimonies they could tell and have told of His undeniable interventions, healings, encounters, and experiences that they, too, have had with the Lord. All of our testimonies are so important. They are not just memories to be treasured; they are evidence of our real Savior and of our faithful Father. They are stories that need to be told!

Experience is a Game-Changer

The experiences along our journey, develop in us a deep-seated faith in God that empowers us to face situations with our focus on Him and not on ourselves. They also give us an ability to become a living testimony that can make known to others the reality of the Lord's power and goodness.

Experience is a game-changer! I once heard a minister say, "A man with an experience is never at the mercy of a man with an opinion." As we walk with the Lord, we will experience His willingness and ability to keep us and make His power known to us, and we will emerge from every circumstance with a stronger confidence and an unshakable faith in God that can only come from experience.

The story of David and Goliath illustrates the difference that having experience with God can make in a person's life. For David, the showdown with Goliath was a defining moment. The destiny inside David had met up with its prophetic timing, and whether he realized it or not, that event wasn't just about defeating a giant; it was a moment that would forever change history. I'm sure that David did not realize the magnitude of the moment he had stepped into, but his past experiences with the Lord had prepared him for the transition that was about to take place. As David heard the giant mocking God and the armies of the Lord, a righteous indignation rose in him that provoked him to take a stand that no one else was willing to take. David wasn't the most qualified. According to men's standards, he wasn't even properly equipped to take on such a fight. But he had courage within him that the others on that hillside did not seem to possess. When David ran into that valley, it was his past experiences with the Lord that became a force that gave him uncommon confidence to face and defeat that giant. David's victory was a testimony of the power and ability of God that provoked faith and hope in all who witnessed that amazing event.

What we have learned about the Lord along our journey is not information that should be forgotten or discarded. Those experiences are "marking moments." They are stories that must be told. Like David, we may tell the stories through our faith responses in critical situations, allowing others to see the evidence of the power and reality of God's protection, goodness, and wisdom demonstrated in undeniable ways. Sometimes, our stories are told as we verbally share them with others, testifying of our unflinching faith in God that has come as a result of our experiences with Him. And then sometimes, God may ask us to gather up our experiences and share them in written form for others to hear, read, and discover His power and goodness through our testimonies. This was the case for me. My Aunt Mot and several people asked me to write about my experiences, but I just never really felt the urgency to do so...until now. I asked the Lord about it, and

I heard Him say, "Write your stories." That was His instruction to me, and so, this book is my response to that instruction.

I pray that it is understood by the reader, but I must insistently state that this book is not about me, and I do not in any way wish to make it so. I know that without the Lord I can do nothing! I will share many personal things that I have experienced along my journey, but it is not my intention to come across as though I am promoting myself. Before writing this book, I shared my concerns about this with the Lord, stating emphatically, "I do not want to make this about me!" to which He answered, "Those experiences that became testimonies happened *to* you, but they are NOT *about* you.... They are all about Me, and it's time to make them known."

It is my prayer that these testimonies will encourage each reader in a deep and profound way. May the words that I write inspire, and may the stories I share prophetically declare to you that what He has done for me, He will do for you.

God is always faithful. He may not work in exactly the same way for every individual. The way He worked through and for me may be different than how He works through and for you, but His power to heal, protect, save, deliver, and guide remains the same. His power is real and available to work in your life and situations to perform His will and intentions in His timing and in His determined ways.

Not every prayer I have prayed and not every act of obedience brought about exactly what I thought should have happened, but I trust that God is sovereign. He sees what we don't see. He knows what we don't know, and if we trust Him and follow His leading, He will work all things according to His plans and intentions, and we will ultimately find that all He does is for our good and for the revealing of His glory.

I once heard author and Bible teacher, Kay Arthur, share an amazing quote. It's so true and so fitting for us to remember when we make the choice to walk by faith in the Lord. Sharing from a note someone, who had been through a very difficult time, had given her, Kay quoted: "Although I cannot explain the [difficulties in life] which strike at us, I do know and trust and rest in the sovereignty of God who is too loving and kind to be cruel and too all-knowing and wise to make a mistake."[2]

It is true that, although we may not understand everything along the journey, still, we can trust that God's leading is always right. So, don't let the "fog" deter you. The ultimate great adventure awaits. Be bold. Be courageous. Trust God. Take those leaps of faith, and experience the fullness of His love and faithfulness along the journey that He has charted for you. The knowing is in the going.

2

Marked by a Moment

In that hour Jesus rejoiced in the Spirit and said, "I thank You, Father, Lord of Heaven and earth, that You have hidden these things from the wise and prudent and revealed them to babes. Even so, Father, for so it seemed good in Your sight."

–Luke 10:21 NKJV

One of the first experiences I had in witnessing the demonstrated power of God happened when I was probably around six years old. Understanding that a memory recalled from a happening at such a young age has the ability to be lacking or maybe even a bit exaggerated in content, I asked my mom about the details, and she (and others) verified the validity of this memory. It is embedded deeper than just in my mind; it is forever branded in my spirit. I am convinced this was a God setup, a necessary event that would help to shape the destiny of a life yet to be lived and a journey yet to be traveled.

Growing up in a small community, there wasn't a lot of excitement, as far as events were concerned. One would have to travel to the larger cities in order to enjoy such outings. However, that summer, there was an event that unfolded that literally marked my life forever.

A large tent that seated hundreds of people was erected in a small town near us. It wasn't the circus that came to town, it was a revival in which the undeniable power of God was put on display for all who came to experience the reality of Jesus! One of the speakers in the revival was Dr. T. L. Lowery, a nationally known revivalist. Hundreds gathered from near and far to attend that meeting. The sick, the lost, the bound, and the saints desiring more came with an expectation that created an atmosphere in which God would come and demonstrate His love and might.

My momma and daddy loaded up my brother and me, and along with my grandparents and some other family members, we all made our way to the meeting. I remember being fascinated by the size of the tent and the number of people who had gathered there. I had never seen that many people in one location. It was a bit overwhelming for a six-year-old, so I stayed close to my daddy.

The seats were arranged in such a way that one section was situated next to the right side of the stage, and that is where my family chose to sit. As a small child, that stage appeared to be extremely high. I was just mesmerized by all that was happening. I don't remember anything about the message that Dr. Lowery preached, but I vividly remember the moments that followed the message.

An invitation was given to any and all who wanted to come and have Dr. Lowery pray for them. Instantly, a line began to form that stretched all the way around the back of the tent. Hundreds got into the line, my family among them.

Momma and Daddy left us in our section with the strict instructions that we were not to leave our seats. They then took their place in the line, being almost the very last ones. Not realizing the powerful things that were happening, my brother, my cousins, and I were fairly bored as we waited for the return of our family members. The line seemed to be moving very slowly as Dr. Lowery prayed over each person who came forward.

I'm not sure who the instigator actually was—I'm pretty sure it was my brother—but in our bored state of mind, someone dared me to go up on that stage. Just in front of our seats were steps leading up to the side of the platform. The dare was to go up the steps onto the stage and then come back to my seat. In an attempt to appear as the brave one among us, I took the dare. I slowly made my way up the steps and found myself standing on the edge of the platform. As I returned to my seat, I was proud of my accomplishment but quickly found that my courageous act had only partially impressed the others. Then came the "double-dog" dare to go all the way out to the podium. Well, what's a girl to do? I couldn't chicken out now! So, with trembling knees, I made my way out to the center of the stage and stood behind the pulpit where Brother Lowery had just delivered his fiery sermon.

It was my intention just to run up the steps, cross the stage, touch the podium and then run back across the stage, down the steps, and return to my seat. However, just as I turned to run back to my seat after having touched the podium, what was happening down in the altar area captured my attention. The power of God was moving on people's bodies and lives, and people were testifying of instant miracles. I saw people rejoicing, crying, falling onto the ground under the weight of indescribable glory. I can't articulate it completely, and though I didn't understand it all at the time, I was captivated by Holy Spirit in that moment. It was as if what God was doing in the lives of those people was the only thing that was happening in the whole world. I was completely awestruck!

Suddenly, I felt a hand on my shoulder, and that amazing moment came to a screeching halt! Someone who worked with the crusade team had observed my mischievous behavior and had come to lead me back to my seat. I think that may have been the first time in my life that I felt the icy grip of fear!

Just as she took my hand to begin to escort me off the stage, Brother Lowery, who was down in the altar area praying over the people, spun around and saw me, and in his deep, anointed voice, he said to the lady, "Leave her alone! Let her stay there and watch. God said that she needs to see what's happening here. She is going to need this someday." He then looked me in the eyes and said, "Honey, you stay right there and watch what God does here! You will never forget this."

I stood next to that pulpit, and I watched as people were healed from cancer, delivered from demons, saved, and baptized in the Holy Ghost. I saw my own parents supernaturally touched by the power of God. I witnessed supernatural miracles, signs, and wonders, one after the other. Too many stories to tell. The power of God that manifested that night was indescribable! I don't know that my six-year-old mind could have fully comprehended the magnitude of what was happening there, but one thing is for certain: I understood enough to know that what I was seeing was from God. From the vantage point of that high stage, I was given an opportunity to witness the demonstration of the undeniable ability of God to touch lives and change the unchangeable.

An innocent dare to go onto that platform literally led me into a defining moment that set the stage for the future that God had destined for my life. I had no idea of the journey that lay ahead of me, but God did, and He created that moment in order to introduce me to His mighty power! Dr. Lowery's prophetic decree over me was right on. I needed what I saw there, and I have never forgotten it. Those miracles are forever branded in my spirit.

God is leading each of us according to the plans that He has purposed for our lives. He sees what we don't see, and He knows what we don't know, but if we will surrender to and trust Him, we will find that He has injected into our journey necessary, defining moments that have the power to reveal Him to us. For those of us who are born again, we have access to God (see Hebrews 4:14-16), and as we focus on Him, He will position us with divine vantage points that allow us to witness the reality of His power and person. He beckons to us all, "Stand still and see My salvation." For the more that we see Him, the more our hearts are forged with unshakeable faith and confidence in Him.

Dr. Lowery knew God. He was confident in the power of Holy Spirit to work through him to reveal the reality of God's love and power to those for whom he prayed. Dr. Lowery availed himself to God, and through Him, God worked in miraculous ways. Those miracles not only changed the lives of those who received them, but they formed an image of God in my six-year-old mind that has never diminished. That image helped to form a foundation of faith in God upon which I have chosen to build my life.

3

Have Faith in God

"For My thoughts are not your thoughts, nor are your ways My ways," says the Lord. "For as the heavens are higher than the earth, so are My ways higher than your ways, and My thoughts than your thoughts."

—Isaiah 55:8, 9 NKJV

Our journey with the Lord is a journey of faith. It begins with faith in God, and it effectively continues as we maintain that faith in God. Faith is a message that has been severely misconstrued. It is often believed that faith is a feeling that we have to work up when we need something from God. Faith is more than a feeling; it is steadfast belief and confidence in God!

The successful fulfillment of the journey that God has planned for our lives cannot be realized without Him. He designed us to need Him. He desires not just that we know about Him, but that we know Him. We get to know Him through spending time reading the Bible, hearing the

Word, communicating with Him in prayer (listening and not just asking), and hearing the testimonies of His awesome power and ability from others. The more we know Him, the more we will trust Him.

"Let us therefore come boldly to the throne of grace, that we may obtain mercy and find grace to help in time of need" (Hebrews 4:16 KJV). In this verse, the word help means to aid or to assist.[1]

When I was a child, our family would go camping every summer. Often on these excursions, we would do a lot of walking. At times, being so small, I would get so tired that my daddy would pick me up, put me on his shoulders, and carry me. What a relief it would be to get off my feet and rest on the strength of his shoulders! I would still be moving toward the goal, but it was Daddy's strength that was making it possible.

Oftentimes in our lives, we become overwhelmed by the goings on around us. We become weary in life and desire to just sit down and quit. But we have a purpose for living, and if we stop, that purpose will never be accomplished. The great thing about God is, He hasn't asked us to walk through this life by our own strength and ability. He invites us to come boldly into His presence to find and obtain mercy, compassion, and divine influence that will aid and assist in our times of need. What an awesome invitation!

I don't know why we choose to carry so much weight around with us—worries, fears, insecurities, doubts, stress, etc.—trying to manage on our own, when God is more than able to give us the assistance, the help we need! Why don't we just stop doing it on our own and climb up on His strength? What a relief it is to release it all to Him! We'll still be moving toward the goal, but now His strength will be enabling us to get there!

Faith Over Fear

Testimonies are the result of our experiences in the "tests" of life. Many people want the testimonies without the trials and tests, but it is actually during the difficult times that we see and experience God's hand at work on our behalf. It's not that God creates the difficulties to somehow "teach us a lesson." He's a good Father. Satan comes to steal, to kill, and to destroy. However, it is in those times (when satan intends to use the difficulties to separate us from our faith in God) that if we stay focused on and trust the Lord, we will rise up with a testimony of the overcoming power of God.

Jesus said, "In the world you will have tribulation, but be of good cheer; I have overcome the world" (John 16:33 NKJV). In this text, the word *tribulation* refers "to pressure and trouble." We are in the world, and in this life we will face times of pressure and struggle. But, as born-again heirs of God, the Bible teaches us that we are in Christ. Paul reveals in Galatians 2:20 that we have been crucified with Christ, and it is no longer we who live, but Christ lives in us. The life that we now live in the flesh, we live by faith in the Son of God, who loved us and gave Himself for us.

Yes, in the world we will face times of pressure and difficult situations, but though we are in the world, we are more so in Christ, and in Christ, we have the power to overcome because He overcame the world. The one key advantage that we have as Christians in this world is our faith in God.

Some people struggle with the issue of faith because they have developed a misplaced focus that is often the product of fear. When fear is given a place in our thought processes, it draws our attention off God and causes us to focus on ourselves, our circumstances, our understanding or lack thereof, our finances or lack thereof, our ability or lack thereof, other people's opinions and expectations, etc. This misplaced focus will bring us to the conclusion that we're not really hearing from God at all.

Fear is often one of the biggest obstacles that must be overcome when learning to walk by faith. It is a deceptive snare that works in opposition to faith, and if allowed, fear will capture your courage and shroud you in the confinement of emotional reasoning.

Fear and faith are both presented to us every day, every step of our journey, and we each have to choose where we place our trust. One choice leads to undiscovered potential and purpose; the other leads to living the life God created us to live. He instructs us to "choose life" (see Deuteronomy 30:19). Choose faith in God!

God's ways are not our ways, and His thoughts are not our thoughts (see Isaiah 55:8-9). He sees beyond the scope of our human ability. Faith in God allows us to focus beyond ourselves and trust in His ability and faithfulness, even when doing so is not logical to our natural understanding. This is critically important for our journey because there are going to be times when God leads us in ways that make absolutely no sense to our natural minds, and it is by faith alone that we will trust Him and follow Him beyond the boundaries of our own strength and understanding. That's why we must not be driven by our emotions, but we must be anchored in confident faith in God.

4

Persuaded Faith

But he did not doubt or waver in unbelief concerning the promise of God, but he grew strong and empowered by faith, giving glory to God, being fully convinced that God had the power to do what He had promised.

—Romans 4:20, 21 AMP

For Christians, the journey of faith begins with believing in God and accepting Jesus Christ as our Lord and Savior, but it doesn't end there. God wants us to keep moving from the foundational doctrines of Christ into a mature and confident persuasion that He is who He says He is, that He has what He says He has, and that He will do what He says He can do. That growth and maturity comes as we humble ourselves to walk with Him. The journey allows us to discover more and more about the Lord, and those discoveries build and form within us an unshakeable trust in the One who has saved us and calls us His own.

The enemy of our souls, and sometimes, even our own flesh, will try to convince us that devoting our lives to the Lord is way too complicated, and even an unachievable goal, but it's not complicated at all. It's a matter of focus. This is why the Word instructs us to "[Look] unto Jesus, the Author and Finisher of our faith" (see Hebrews 12:2). When He becomes our focus and when our priority is to know and follow Him, then our lives begin to revolve around Him. Walking with Him becomes a naturally supernatural way of life.

Prayer, time spent reading the Word of God, and praying in the Spirit helps us to become familiar with and recognize His voice. Hearing and knowing that we have heard from the Lord creates a confidence that enables us to look beyond ourselves and obey His leading. It's not so much that we feel that we are bold and courageous based on our own merit. As a matter of fact, on the inside, we may tremble with uncertainty. But when we know that He has spoken–regardless of what may seem to be lacking on our part where the assignment is concerned–faith empowers us to trust and obey Him, anyway. We obey, not necessarily because we can see the way or figure out the details, but simply because we are confident that God is with us, that His Spirit is in us, and that He is faithful to do through us that which we cannot do on our own. This is the Word of the Lord: "It's not by might, nor by power, but by My Spirit."

A Lesson Learned

Several years ago, I was attending a "School of the Spirit" class at a local church. In the class, we were learning about the power of God and the necessity of its operation in and through our lives as believers. One of my assignments in the class was to read a book that was written by Norvel Hayes. I don't remember the title of the book, but the content was all about the demonstrated healing power of Jesus. The author gave many testimonies of how he had witnessed the power of God in his own life and how that same power had worked through him as he had prayed for others.

I had known that healing was real. I had witnessed the evidence of the Lord's healing power in my own body and in others around me. We had attended meetings in which we had witnessed amazing miracles as God worked through men of faith, like R.W. Shambach, T.L. Lowery, and others. We, ourselves, believed the Word of God and the reality of its truth being demonstrated. We saw and heard testimonies in our little church of how God healed and worked supernaturally in many situations. However, our prayers for healing and the miraculous intervention of God were many times laced with hope, and not so much with persuaded expectation. Norvel Hayes spoke of the outcomes of persuaded faith, and his words awakened a deep desire in me to know God as he knew Him and to have that same kind of faith in God.

I once heard someone say, "Prayer is a door of access to the fullness of God, and faith is the key that unlocks the door." Profound! The key of faith is more than hope; it is persuasion and undaunted confidence in God that fuels effectual and fervent prayers that avail much.

In Romans 4:3, Paul said that Abraham "believed God." Verse twenty-one of that same chapter says that Abraham was "fully persuaded that what [God] promised, He was able also to perform." What Abraham possessed was more than just a casual hope that God would fulfill His promises; he was persuaded that God would and could keep His word. That confident belief in God impacted how he lived his life, and through him, the evidence of God's power was manifested and gave testimony of the reality of that power, not only to his generation but even to us today!

As I read the book by Norvel Hayes, the reality of persuaded faith somehow clicked on the inside of me, and I remember so vividly what I did at that moment when that light of revelation came on!

For many days my mom had been suffering terribly with back pain. She had been in bed because it was too excruciating to get up and move about. Captured by the truth of what I was reading in that book, I literally threw the book down on my bed, and I said out loud, "Okay! God, if what this minister is saying is true—that we can pray with unwavering confidence that You will do what Your Word says You will do—then I need to know that! I need that deep, unwavering faith in You to come alive in me. So, if this is true—and I believe it is—then I ask that you would heal my momma today."

I wasn't being disrespectful to God. A deep longing had been stirred in me. I was so hungry to know God and to have all that He intended for me to have. At that moment, I felt the power of God come over me. I went out of my room to go and lay my hands on Momma and pray for her. I went to her room, but she wasn't there! I went down the hall and heard her in the shower. God had touched her! She said that she just decided she was going to get up out of that bed, and from that moment on, she was totally healed!

God did not have to prove Himself to me, yet, for my sake, He allowed me to have visible evidence and confirmation that ensured me that I can know His will. I can pray in agreement with Him with unwavering faith in Him and trust that He will perform the doing of what He said.

F. F. Bosworth once said, "Faith begins where the will of God is known."[1] This is made clear in 1 John 5:14-15: "Now this is the confidence that we have in Him, that if we ask anything according to His will, He hears us. And if we know that He hears us, whatever we ask, we know that we have the petitions that we have asked of Him." Knowing the will of God provokes confident faith that opens the door for supernatural happenings.

We see this demonstrated in the life of Jesus. He said that He could do nothing of Himself, except what He saw the Father do, and whatever He saw the Father do, He would do likewise (see John 5:19). In another instance, He said that He spoke what the Father told Him to speak (see John 12:49-50). Jesus knew the will of the Father, and that knowing enabled Him to operate in confident faith in God. He aligned His actions and expectations with God's will, and powerful things were accomplished.

How do we know what God's will is? As I have previously stated, prayer and the Word of God are necessary components when it comes to hearing God and knowing His will. Oftentimes, Holy Spirit will speak to us during those times of prayer and study, and also during times of fasting. The will of God is sometimes revealed through trusted prophetic voices, sermons, dreams, or visions. God can speak to us in various ways, but the key way to hear and know His will is to spend time with Him in worship and prayer.

The Lord will make known to us His desires, and when we know His will and are fully persuaded that God will do what He says, then we can become a co-laborer with Jesus Christ and with Holy Spirit. God will work in us, for us, and through us to do "great things and unsearchable, marvelous things without number" (Job 5:9).

When the disciples asked Jesus how He did what He did, His answer was, "Have faith in God" (Mark 11:22).

To walk the path that God has ordained for our lives, we must have this persuaded faith. There are going to be times when the Lord will lead us to specific assignments or ask us to do certain things that we may not have the resources or even the understanding to do, but part of the joy of the journey will be experienced as we trust and obey Him anyway. When we are persuaded that God is trustworthy—so much so that we trust Him beyond our own natural capabilities—that is confident faith. And confident faith in God opens the door of access into the treasure of His exceeding, abundantly above all that we could ask, think, or imagine.

You are Not a Victim

Several years ago, some friends and I were sharing a home that we were renting. We had been there for a few years. Each month the rent had been paid—not one payment had ever been missed or late—and we had meticulously taken care of the property. One day, out of the blue, a neighbor came by to tell us that he saw in the newspaper that our home was to be auctioned! We were completely shocked! We later found that the people we were paying our rent to had not been paying the mortgage, so the house had gone into foreclosure. They never even bothered to tell us!

Even though the foreclosure was from no fault of ours, we had to go to court and were told that we would have to vacate the property. We were given a thirty-day notice. We had no idea what to do or where to go, so we prayed. One of my friends received an absolute knowing that God had a really good place for us and that He would make a way for us to get into it. We did not know where the place was or when or how He would lead us to it, but, like Abraham, my friend believed God, and she was fully persuaded that He would provide.

A couple of days after our court appearance, a policeman showed up at the house to serve the eviction notice. My friends were outside, mowing the yard. The policeman was taken aback at how the place looked so nice and well-kept. He said that most places where he went to serve eviction notices were just trashed. When he asked my friend where we were going to move, she told him, “We don’t know yet, but God has a really good place for us. I wish you could see what He will do for us!” Convinced, he stated that he wished he could, too.

We didn’t just sit around doing nothing about our situation. We searched diligently for another place to live, but no matter what we did on our own, nothing seemed to work.

Our neighbors knew of our situation, one of which would walk by or drive by and see us outside, and she would holler, “Do you know where you’re going yet?” My friend would confidently reply, “No, but God has a really good place for us. You just watch and see!” This happened several times.

Weeks passed, and the time for us to move was getting nearer. The closer the day came, the more the enemy tried to make us doubt our position of faith in God. Human nature wants to jump up and "fix it." But the spirit man says, "Wait upon the Lord."

One day, I found myself feeling really down. I couldn't understand why this was happening to us. It just didn't seem fair! Suddenly, I heard the Lord speak to me as clearly as I had ever heard Him! It wasn't an audible voice that I heard, but it was so clear that it may as well have been. It was one of those moments when, as one older minister once said, "It felt like my whole body became an ear!" The Lord said to me, "You are NOT a victim, and don't you act like one! I am working in all of this, and the outcome will be for your good and for My glory!" I told my friends what I had heard, and together, we rejoiced, knowing that God was going to work through our situation to make His glory known!

A few days later, one of my friends and I felt led of the Lord to go to the Red River Meeting House near Russellville, Kentucky and pray about this situation. This was the first time we had ever gone to that historic location. When we stepped into that small meeting house, we could feel such a sweet presence of the Lord. As we prayed, I heard the Lord say, "Watch the river. When the river rises, you will know that I have risen to the occasion." I had no idea what that meant, but I spoke it out loud, and I wrote it down.

The date we were set to move was on a Monday, and it was just over one week after the Lord had given me that word to watch the river. On Friday and Saturday, before we were to move, just under fourteen inches of rain fell in our area, causing massive flooding. The Cumberland River rose to unheard-of levels as the rain fell, overflowing its banks and flooding many parts of the city of Clarksville and many areas throughout our county. It was a historic event for our county and for many places in the state of Tennessee. The news headline that morning was "The River is Rising."

We still had no idea where we were going or what to do, but God's promise was that when the river rose, we would know that He had risen to the occasion! Now, the river had risen, and we were confident that He would fulfill His promise! The flood wasn't the Lord's doing, but it just "happened" to come at the same time we were to move. It was an undeniable sign to us that what had felt like an impossible situation was now becoming a turning of events in our favor.

We had rented a moving truck, and we were scheduled to pick it up that Saturday morning. It was chaotic as we were trying to maneuver in the rain and through the city to get to the pick-up location, but the Lord gave us favor and guided us there and back. We parked the very large truck in the driveway at our house and began the process of packing and preparing to move. As we were loading things onto the truck, that unbelieving neighbor drove by, rolled down her window, and with a smirky grin on her face and a giggle in her voice, she said, "Do you know where you're going yet?"

My friend was unshaken. She said, "No, but God has a really good place for us, you just watch and see!"

The next day, on Sunday morning, I was scheduled to speak at a church in our area. It was a difficult time for so many. Some had lost their homes, others had lost their businesses, and there had even been loss of life due to the horrific flooding. I felt a strong anointing that morning as I spoke, and I shared with the people that we can still trust God! We may not understand everything, but we CAN trust God.

I came home that afternoon, and we continued packing the moving truck. We packed that truck like we knew exactly where we were going!

While I was inside the house packing up a few last-minute things, a man strolled into the front yard and struck up a conversation with my friends. He asked why we were moving, and they told him the whole story. He asked where we were going, to which they replied, "We don't know, but God has a good place for us! You just watch and see." The man seemed kind of taken aback by that response. He then told them that he had a house in the neighborhood that he was trying to sell. He invited them to go and look at it. They asked him the price, and it was way out of our range, and they told him so! He still insisted that they at least come and look at it. As they were walking through the house, the man told them that he would be willing to rent it to us, but again, his price was too much for our budget. So, without telling him how much we could afford, they told him how grateful they were for his consideration, but they had to politely refuse his offer. He said, "Well, if something doesn't open up for you by morning, contact me and we'll talk about it and see what we can do." He gave them his phone number, and then he was gone. We had never met this man before.

The next morning, the day we had to be out of the house, the last things to load were our beds and personal items. As we were about to leave, the man came back to our house. He began to cry and said, "I wasn't able to sleep much last night! For some time now, I've been asking the Lord to teach me how to hear His voice. Yesterday, I heard Him. He told me that I was supposed to rent my house to you as long as you need it!" He told us the amount he felt he was to ask us to pay. That amount was only ten dollars more than what we had previously been paying for rent!

We immediately moved into the new place. It was a beautiful home...an answer to faith-filled prayer.

Confident faith in God carried us through that difficult time and kept us focused on Him. It was a trying time, and while He didn't deliver us *from* the storm, He did deliver us *in* the storm...literally! He worked and proved His faithfulness, even to our skeptical, unbelieving neighbor! God rose to the occasion, and He turned things for our good–even when it seemed impossible–and He received much glory!

We have been able to tell that story to many people over the years, and to this day, God still uses it to encourage others. This is not a story about our strength and ability! There was nothing we could do. It is a story of the power of confident faith and the ability of our loving Father.

In his writings to Timothy, the apostle Paul said, "Fight the good fight of faith..." (see 1 Timothy 6:12 KJV). My friend and assistant, Darlene, once heard a powerful and enlightening word from the Lord. He said to her, "To stand, therein lies the fight." When you know that you have heard from God, stand, and when you've done all that you can to stand, just keep standing. Stand with full persuasion that what God has promised, He is able also to perform! Confident faith in God is the victory that overcomes!

This is a step-by-step journey, but every step we take by faith will give us invaluable experiences that reveal more and more about God. We grow as we go. I have certainly experienced the reality of this truth in my own life.

5

The Impact of Demonstrated Faith

"You are the light of the world. A city that is set on a hill cannot be hidden. Nor do they light a lamp and put it under a basket, but on a lampstand, and it gives light to all who are in the house. Let your light so shine before men, that they may see your good works and glorify your Father in Heaven."

–Matthew 5:14-16 NKJV

"I don't want to go around the curve." I was maybe seven years old, and my cousins and I were riding our bicycles down our grandparents' driveway. At the very end of the drive was a slight curve that led to the main road where we would turn around and make our way back up the hill to the shade tree where we would stop and rest as though we had been on a long journey.

We had made this trip many times, but for some reason, I didn't want to go around the curve that day.

Something inside me told me not to go. My cousins, however, went on ahead. It was only a matter of maybe a minute that they came running back up the driveway without their bicycles. They were crying and screaming, "*Pawpaw is on fire*! PAWPAW IS ON FIRE!"

Our grandpa had been working on a car that had stalled at the end of the driveway. To get the car to start, he had been priming the carburetor by pouring gasoline into it. During this process, the engine backfired, and the gasoline ignited, leaving my grandpa with severe burns on his hands, arms, and face.

As my cousins ran to the house to inform our grandma and others, I decided to walk around the curve. I arrived in time to see grandpa removing his shirt in order to snuff out the flames. His hair was singed, and portions of his skin were hanging from his hands, arms, and face.

I ran to his side, crying. He calmly said, "Let's go to the house." And that's what we did. We entered the house to find that Grandma was crying and very scared for Grandpa. Fear had already made its entrance into her mind just from hearing the news of what had happened, but seeing him in this horrible condition exacerbated the intensity of it.

"What are we going to do?" she frantically cried.

I will never forget Grandpa's words to her. It was more of a statement of faith than a response. He said, "We can pray!" And pray they did!

Then they took him to the emergency room at a local hospital. The doctors debrided all of the multiple, severe burns. They gave him a prescription for pain medications and told him to go by the pharmacy and get the prescription filled. His response to that was, "I won't need it." They replied, "O, you will definitely need it."

But he didn't.

My grandpa was a man who completely trusted God. He didn't just believe that God exists; He believed that God was, is, and always will be almighty, and that He would always be faithful to keep His Word. Grandpa was a simple man. Born in 1906, he had witnessed his share of hard times. His father had died from an influenza outbreak when Grandpa was a teenager, so he had to grow up very quickly. He began working as a coal miner and eventually became a farmer. He didn't have an education. He couldn't read and could barely write enough to sign his own name. He asked God to help him learn to read the Bible, and the Lord answered that prayer. He loved the Word of God, and He loved the God of the Word. He modeled a life that exemplified his love for and trust in the Lord. Everyone who knew him knew about God and about Jesus—of this he made sure!

So, in the face of this horrific incident, when given the choice to be afraid or to trust God, Grandpa chose to trust God. And why would he *not* trust Him? His track record had proven Him to be faithful time and time again!

To the amazement of everyone, those burns completely healed. He never even had a scar from them. If he had pain, we never knew about it. God supernaturally kept him and healed him. What was a horrible accident that could have led to debilitation or even death, was turned into a testimony of the power of faith in God. Everyone knew it had to be God. There was no other explanation.

My life was profoundly impacted by that miracle. The healing power of Jesus had become more than just a Sunday School story demonstrated with flannelgraphs. (If you know, you know!) It was real! I had witnessed God's miraculous power at work in and through my grandpa. I saw faith in action, and that moment is forever imbedded in my memory and has served as a constant reminder throughout my life that God is real and that He is Healer. He is faithful, and He is trustworthy!

Though we may not always understand the happenings in our lives, still through it all, we can trust God to lead us. He is a faithful Father, and our decision to trust and follow Him gives Him access into our lives to work according to His will for His glory and for our good.

I am not saying that everyone's experience has to be exactly the same as my grandpa's experience. God leads people in various ways to bring healing and help to them. In some situations, God may use the hands of a doctor or a surgeon to bring healing. Sometimes healing will be instant, and other times it may be a process. God works in different ways. But what I am saying is that when we follow Him, however He leads, He will work in and through our lives, giving evidence of His power. In turn, our experiences with the Lord create a testimony, a story that can be told to impact others on their journey. Just as my grandpa's decision to trust God opened the way for him to encounter the Lord in a very powerful way, the testimony that was birthed from that experience touched many other lives, including mine...and now, even yours.

Faith in God gives Him an open door to appropriate His will, power, wisdom, and ability in and through our lives. As a born-again believer, our life is meant to be lived as a testimony that reveals the reality of Jesus to the world around us. We are His witnesses. We know Him, and we are called to make Him known.

The greatest gift we can give to those being influenced by our lives is to allow Jesus to be seen in us as He works for us and through us. The joy of the journey is that we can experience Christ in His fullness and therefore become a light that illuminates a path that will lead others to Him.

6

The Tangible Power of God

"Electricity is God's power in the natural realm, but the Holy Ghost is God's power in the spirit realm."

–John G. Lake

The first time I remember feeling and experiencing the tangible presence of God rushing through my physical body was when I was around seven years old. My mom and dad had taken us to a revival meeting that was taking place at a small church in our area. I don't remember who the preacher was, nor do I remember his sermon, but I do remember what I felt that night as though it happened yesterday.

I was sitting on the second pew with my family and some friends. At one point in the meeting, the Holy Spirit suddenly began to move with such power that people just began rushing to the altar. Many of my young friends were being deeply touched by the Lord. I stood up to see what was happening, and I was instantly gripped by the power of God. It wasn't a "worked-up emotion," nor was it fake. It felt like electricity was shooting all through my body, and I grabbed hold of the seat in front of me to keep myself from collapsing to the floor. The minister saw what was happening to me, and he came over and asked if I wanted to come to the altar and pray. I shook my head no. I was afraid to move.

At first, I didn't fully understand what was happening to me, but I remember watching my friends, who were being so impacted by Holy Spirit, and I knew it was He who was touching me, as well. I was overwhelmed with the understanding that Jesus was real and He was near, and I have never forgotten the tangible power that accompanied His presence. I have known and experienced His tangible power many times throughout my life, but that first encounter was a marking moment that helped to set the course of my journey with the Lord.

A Wave of Glory

One year, I attended a week-long camp meeting. Thousands of people gathered for those meetings, and during that time, we saw and experienced many powerful things. One particular night, I remember there was such a holy moment that we entered into. The minister was speaking, and suddenly, he began to say, "The Lord is doing something up there in that section of the building." The building was very large, with thousands of seats, and every seat was filled. It was a round building, and the minister was pointing to a section in the upper left side from where he stood. This wasn't a fake, "work-up-the-crowd" kind of thing; it was so holy.

Suddenly, there was a visible cloud that appeared in the very section he was pointing to, and that cloud began to move like a wave across that entire building. As it moved, some of those under it began to fall to the floor. Others shook under the power of God, and some ran around the building as they were impacted by the glory of God. I watched in awe as that wave of glory moved across that congregation, and I felt His power as it moved over me. It was the same tangible power I had felt in that little country church when I was seven years old.

Later that night, there were testimonies of healings, deliverances, and powerful encounters with the Lord that had been experienced as the cloud moved above us. God had come among us and had made Himself known.

The Fiery Glory

Another experience I had with the tangible glory of God happened one night after a Sunday evening meeting at our church. It had been a powerful gathering. It was one of those meetings when we felt the power and goodness of God moving among us, and we didn't want to leave. Those types of experiences are hard to explain. It's one of those things where you would have to have been there to fully understand. But to those who have experienced it, you never forget it!

Not long after we had returned home from the meeting that evening, we received a telephone call saying that our church building was on fire. We immediately got in the car and went back to the church! There were firetrucks in front of the building, and there were firefighters with hoses inside. Eyewitnesses had seen smoke and flames coming out of the attic vent at the end of the church building, and apparently, the smoke was still visible when the firemen arrived. After several moments, one of the firemen came out and announced that there was no fire, and there were no signs of a physical fire anywhere to be found inside the building. They were puzzled by this and said assuredly that they were still searching to be sure they just hadn't overlooked something in the attic. Nothing was ever found to give a natural reason for the smoke and flames. The Fire was not natural; it was supernatural. Like Moses of old, the visible Fire of the presence of God had come and burned, but it did not consume. Everyone was aware of that fact, believers and non-believers alike.

The Impact of Divine Encounters

These unexplainable accounts may seem foolish and even unbelievable to some, but as the song declares, "Mine eyes have seen the glory." These and many other powerful moments like them have left a permanent impact on my life. God desires to make Himself known to us.

All through the Bible we find accounts of people who had real encounters with the Lord. Their lives were powerfully changed, and their God-ordained destinies were launched as these encounters led them to the undeniable realization that God is real, Christ is real, and Holy Spirit is real.

I think of Saul, who was later named Paul. He was chosen by God, yet didn't know it. He had chosen to live his life as an intimidator and even as a murderer of Christians. Chapter nine in Acts reveals his story. As the chapter unfolds, we find that Saul was on his way to Damascus to see if he could find any "in the Way" so that he might bring them bound back to Jerusalem (see Acts 9:1, 2 KJV). This was his plan; however, the Word of God teaches us that "A man's heart plans his way, but the Lord directs his steps" (Proverbs 16:9 NKJV). Saul had planned his trip to Damascus, but the Lord was ordering his steps right into the throes of a divine encounter that would change the course of his whole life. God already knew the plan He had for this man, and the time had come for that plan to unfold. So, a pre-planned trip led him into a God-ordained moment that launched him into an unforeseen destiny. God changed Saul's name and his trajectory. A holy and divine encounter with the Lord awakened in him a voice that would impact his time and even future generations with the wisdom and revelation of Jesus Christ.

I had no idea that God's plan for my life was unfolding at the times I had all of these encounters that I experienced, but God was equipping me to walk with Him in the days and years ahead. What He was leading me into would require that I know Him by experience. And like Paul, I have never forgotten those encounters with the reality of Jesus. The years that have followed have not been filled with perfection on my part, but my experiences with the Lord have kept me seeking Him and desiring to lay aside every weight and sin that would seek to ensnare me. With my focus and heart set on Him, I deeply desire to run with endurance the race that He has set before me (see Hebrews 12:1).

It's the same for us all. He wants us to know that He is more than just a story or someone else's experience. Intellectual knowledge of the Lord is necessary and foundational, but accompanying the intellectual knowledge must be experiential knowledge that leaves no doubt that God is real, that His plans for our lives are real, and that He is a present and able guide. When Job encountered the Lord, he said, "I have heard of You by the hearing of the ear, but now my eye sees You" (Job 42:5). God wants us to know Him by experience and encounter.

The teachings and the stories that I share in each chapter of this book reveal that we can experience God in tangible ways. Jesus said in Revelation 3:20, "Behold, I stand at the door and knock. If anyone hears My voice and opens the door, I will come in to him and dine with him, and he with Me." He longs for us to open the door of our lives and invite Him to come in and reveal the fullness of His purposes for us and the reality of His Person to us.

When we do that, He enters the door, and when He is truly present, His power is tangible and undeniable.

7

I've Known Him as Healer

"Behold, I Am the Lord, the God of all flesh. Is there anything too hard for Me?"

–Jeremiah 32:27 NKJV

Jehovah Rapha is a name in the Bible used to describe the healing attribute of God. In Hebrew, the word *rapha* means "to mend; to cure,"[1] in essence, to heal. So, Jehovah Rapha means, "I Am [God] who heals." God referred to Himself by this name in Exodus 15:26 when He told the Israelites, "If you diligently heed the voice of the Lord your God and do what is right in His sight, give ear to His commandments and keep all His statutes, I will put none of the diseases on you which I have brought on the Egyptians. For I am the Lord who heals you [Jehovah Rapha]."

God was making a promise to His people that He would bring healing and restoration to all who would be faithful to Him. We find this promise rehearsed throughout the Old Testament.

"Bless the Lord, O my soul, and forget not all His benefits: Who forgives all your iniquities, who heals all your diseases..." (Psalm 103:2-3).

"And the LORD will take away from you all sickness..." (Deuteronomy 7:15).

"He sent His word and healed them and delivered them from their destructions" (Psalm 107:20).

The New Testament reveals to us that Jesus, Yeshua, the Son of God, came to this earth as Emmanuel, God with us. He, who was God incarnate, took on flesh and came to dwell among us. In His earthly life, Yeshua gave Himself as the ultimate sacrifice for our sins. In the moments leading up to His crucifixion, He was tied to a whipping post and was brutally and repeatedly beaten with horrific stripes across His back. His sufferings were beyond any attempt to articulate. Isaiah released the prophetic declaration and the amazing revelation that Jesus went through all of that for us! He was wounded for *our* transgressions, He was bruised for *our* iniquities; the chastisement for *our* peace was upon Him, and by His stripes *we* are healed (see Isaiah 53:5).

Jesus came as God in the flesh, and through His selfless sacrifice, God's attribute, *rapha*, was then made available to all who would receive Christ as Savior.

Following are some personal testimonies of how I have come to know Him as *Jehovah Rapha* in my own life and have watched Him work miraculously in others.

He Still Works Miracles

One of the things that I am most grateful for in my life is my family. I come from a long line of believers who have stood on God's Word and witnessed His undeniable power. My daddy and momma have always been strong influences for me. They didn't just talk about Jesus; they lived their lives in such a way that demonstrated His reality to my brother and me. Their strong faith in the Lord was never an "undercover" thing in our household. They showed us by example that walking by faith in God is a commitment, but it is a commitment that has great reward.

As I am writing this chapter, there are fireworks bursting outside. It's the Fourth of July. The month of July holds great significance for our nation, but it also holds great significance for my family.

On July 4, 1988, we celebrated our nation's independence by shooting fireworks for some of the children in the neighborhood. It was a wonderful time of fun, laughter, fellowship, and awe. But, that year, the celebration was short-lived.

The next evening, I stopped by my parent's house on my way to church. I saw that their car was gone, but I really didn't think anything of it. I just assumed that they must have wanted to get to church early that night. I went into the house to get something, and as I was making my way back out to my car, a neighbor came walking up the driveway. She said, "You need to get to the hospital!

Labron has been in a bad car accident. Your momma and daddy are already there."

It was one of those moments when you feel that someone has punched you in the stomach and every bit of breath that you have in you just goes rushing out! I ran to my car and sped away to the hospital. I walked through the ER doors just in time to see my daddy, with his back to the wall, sliding to the floor, sobbing. My brother, who was almost twenty-two years old at the time, had fallen asleep at the wheel as he was driving home earlier that day. His car ran off the road, striking a tree. His head was slammed into the windshield, breaking every bone in his face and causing severe brain swelling.

I was looking at my daddy and then searching the room for Mom, when out the doors came a stretcher carrying my brother. He was bloody, and his face was completely unrecognizable. There was so much swelling that his facial features were almost non-existent.

An ambulance had taken him to our local, small-town hospital, but there was nothing they could do for him there, so they were transporting him to a larger hospital in Chattanooga. Daddy stood to his feet and hugged me so tightly I thought he would squeeze me in two. Then Momma came over and joined the embrace.

We then went outside and got into the car together and made our way to the larger hospital in Chattanooga. There was complete silence as we drove. There were so many things racing through my mind. *Is he aware of what has happened? Is he alert enough to pray? Will he be alive when we get there?*

When we arrived at Erlanger Hospital in Chattanooga, Tennessee, there were many family members and people from our church who had already gathered in the waiting area of the Emergency Room. I remember walking to the water fountain, and I just collapsed to the floor. The next thing I knew, I awoke to find myself sitting in a chair and hearing our pastor's wife's voice as she was praying for me. Not long after that, a doctor came into the waiting area and asked to speak with us. Daddy, Momma, a couple of other people, and I went into a side room. The doctor said, "I won't sugarcoat it. It's bad." He told us that my brother's brain was swelling rapidly and that they would need to address that quickly. He then said that there was a great possibility that he would not survive the night, and if he did live, he would never be "normal" again.

Faith in God is a powerful force that cannot be adequately articulated. When weights are being piled on to the point of breakage, faith doesn't even take the pressure of the weights into consideration; it just pushes through, and says, "Let's just see what God has to say about that!" Faith flips the coin, and announces, "Don't settle for the facts, there's another side to this story. Go to God and hear the truth!"

I saw that kind of faith rise up in my momma at that moment. Meaning no disrespect to the doctor, yet not concerned about his feelings, either, Momma said, "I am so glad to know that my trust is not in a doctor. My trust is in the Lord!" Enough said!

To the amazement of all of the doctors, not only did my brother live through the night, but in time, he was made whole! It didn't happen immediately, but the healing did become a reality. Faith anchored us on the Rock, Christ Jesus, and though the storm was fierce, our foundation could not be shaken. There were temptations to get into fear and doubt, but God would show up, proving Himself strong, time and time again. We stood on the Word, and God manifested His power!

In the weeks that followed, we saw the hand of God at work for my family and for my brother. There were many "small" miracles along the way that kept us encouraged and moving forward. We even found out later that just minutes after the accident happened, a Christian nurse had driven by and had seen the wreck. She knelt beside the car and prayed, and stayed with my brother until the ambulance arrived. Then, as my brother was being transported to Chattanooga, a spirit-filled doctor heard about the transport and met the ambulance enroute. He climbed aboard to ride with them, and he prayed for him the whole way to the hospital. Prayer, the Word, faith, and Holy Spirit–all these worked together to establish an undeniable testimony that would bring much honor and glory to God.

At the time of this writing, it has been thirty-six years since the accident, and my brother is still alive and well...completely whole. He has two wonderful children and two amazing grandchildren, and he's a pretty awesome big brother, too! I'm so glad to know that God still works miracles!

Never Again

In my younger years, I had terrible allergic reactions to pollens every spring and summer. These reactions would be so bad that, at times, I would be in bed for days with swollen eyes, sneezing, coughing, fever, and lack of strength.

During one of those episodes, I received a phone call from a lady who knew nothing about what was happening with me. She said, "I was just standing at my sink, washing my dishes, and I began to pray for you. I prayed for you to be healed of all allergies, and I am calling to tell you, by faith, that you will never be sick from allergies again." From that moment forward, I never experienced those severe allergy symptoms again.

I have experienced the healing power of the Lord many times throughout my life, and for that, I am so grateful!

An Amazing Miracle

A few years ago, my mom, dad, and I had taken my five-year-old great-niece to the Smoky Mountains for a short vacation. One afternoon, we stopped for a picnic. During our time in the picnic area, it suddenly began to rain. My dad and great-niece had gone for a walk, so I grabbed an umbrella and was hurriedly making my way to them. On the way, I stepped on a very slick spot on the ground, and I fell backward. As I was falling, my instincts led me to reach my arm and hand back to try and catch myself as I hit the ground with great force. When I landed, my elbow hyperextended, and instantly became swollen, and I was in horrific pain. The damage to my elbow was really bad, and it left me unable to fully extend or have full use of my arm.

About four months later, I attended a prayer conference in Branson, Missouri with some of my family and friends. One night, during the conference, the preacher was telling the true story of a young minister in an African nation, who had received an amazing, miraculous healing from the Lord.[2] This minister had been shot in the arm, leaving him with a major injury to his elbow. He had to have surgery, during which he received an artificial elbow. The device he had received was too large and caused the young man a lot of pain.

A few years after the surgery, this young minister had been working tirelessly, all day long and into the evening, serving and ministering to over 130,000 people in his church. That evening he heard the Lord say to him, "You have been working hard for Me. Now I'm going to work for you." At that time, he did not know what the Lord meant by that statement. He went to bed that night, and the next morning he awakened to find that the artificial elbow joint that he had surgically received all those years earlier was now lying on the bed next to him! During the night, God had supernaturally given him a brand-new, natural elbow!

The preacher at the conference told us how the doctors had checked the serial numbers on the artificial joint and had confirmed that it was, indeed, the same one that had been surgically placed in that young minister's arm years before. Then, on the overhead screen, he showed a picture of the artificial elbow that God had removed from the young man's arm.

As I listened to the testimony and saw that picture, I was shocked and amazed. I leaned over and asked my friend, "Did he really say what I just thought I heard him say?" As I asked this question, the conference minister then began to say, "Yes, Sir, Lord, I will do that!" Then he announced that the Lord had just spoken to him and told him that there was someone in the room who had an elbow injury and that God was going to heal them that night. He asked for anyone with such an injury to raise their hand. I looked across the congregation, and though there were several thousand people in the room, no one raised their hand. No one!

I had not even thought about my own injury that I had sustained all those months ago. I was still in shock by this amazing testimony I had just heard! My friend, who knew of my elbow injury, looked at me and said, "I think he's talking about you!" Since the time of my accident, four months earlier, I had not been able to completely straighten my arm at all, and it had caused me much pain. But when my friend said those words, without even thinking about it, I raised my arm into the air to see if I had, in fact, been healed. I wasn't raising my hand for the preacher to see me; I was just testing my elbow to see if I could fully extend my arm. I could only lift it a little bit, but it was enough for the preacher to see my experimental test, and he announced, "There you are! You are healed in Jesus' Name!"

At that very moment, though painful at first, my arm extended for the first time in months. I lifted it higher, overcome with joy and amazement, and suddenly all the pain left. People began to clap and rejoice with me. I was totally healed! It was an instant miracle. I had not expected it that night. I wasn't even thinking about my elbow at all, but the Lord touched me, and I was made completely whole!

A couple of years later, I was giving that testimony one night in a meeting where I was speaking. I had not planned to give the testimony, but I felt such a strong prompting of the Lord to do so. After the service, five people came to me to tell me that while I was sharing my testimony, they were instantly healed of various issues! All glory to God!

Right Before Our Eyes

I have witnessed many amazing things through the years. The demonstration of the miraculous power of God is real and life-changing, especially when you watch the miracles take place instantly, right before your eyes.

On one occasion, I was asked to assist a minister as she was praying for people in a prayer line. The minister was standing in front of the people, praying for them, one by one. As she passed quickly by them, she would gently lay her hand on their forehead and say, "Be healed, in the name and the authority of Jesus Christ." That was it. Then she would go on to the next person in line. I was standing behind those for whom she was praying, and directly in front of me stood a lady with a very large, very visible mass that spanned from her throat area to the back of her neck. It was obvious that she was experiencing a lot of pain and discomfort. The minister approached the lady, laid her hand gently on her forehead and said, "Be healed, in the name and the authority of Jesus Christ," and then she continued on to the next person. I remember thinking, *This lady needs serious prayer, not just a gentle touch on the forehead!* I turned for only a second to see what was happening with the next person in the line when I heard a startling scream coming from the lady in front of me—the one for whom the minister had just prayed. She was jumping up and down. She had her hand on the back of her neck, and when she moved her hand, I saw that the huge mass was completely gone! The lady was weeping and rejoicing, declaring, "I'm healed! Thank You, Jesus. I am healed!"

An Instant Miracle

On another occasion, I was with a mission team in a foreign country. We were having meetings in the evenings in one village, and during the day, we separated into small teams and walked throughout that and other surrounding villages to invite people to the evening meetings. As our team of four was walking along the dirt road, we heard a faint voice crying out. It sounded like someone was in distress. We realized the voice was coming from behind a small hut, so we walked into that area and found an older lady lying on the ground. She had fallen and had badly damaged her knee. She had been there for hours in excruciating pain. Her knee was terribly swollen and bruised. Two young men with our team helped her up from the ground to a large log where she could sit down. Her knee was either dislocated or broken. She was crying and afraid.

She told us through an interpreter that as she was lying there all of those hours, she had prayed and asked the Lord to send help. No one was in the area, but she continued to cry out. She said that she knew the Lord had sent us there for her.

We asked if we could pray for her, and she said, "Please do!" One of the young men on our team was a new Christian. He was native to this country and lived in a village nearby. He knelt down on one knee and put his hand very gently on the lady's swollen knee and prayed a simple prayer, "God, please help this lady. Heal her knee." We agreed with him as he prayed. Then, instantly, right before our eyes, every bit of the swelling and all of the bruising went away. Though we had faith in God, the change was so sudden, we were all in amazement. The lady stood up, raised her hands and began to praise the Lord. We all rejoiced with her!

She walked over a mile to the church that night and attended the meeting. She gave her testimony, and we assured the people of the validity of the story. Many were touched by the power of God as He moved through that meeting that night.

A Desperate Moment

A couple of years ago, while driving back home from a ministry assignment where I had preached at a gathering at a church in another state, I began to notice that something didn't feel quite right in my body. With each passing mile, I could feel the undeniable symptoms of some sort of virus that was developing in me. These symptoms worsened and remained in me for a couple of weeks, and then I began to feel better. I thought the sickness had passed, and I was grateful because it was around Christmas time and I had a lot to get done.

The week after I began to feel better, I delved into the swirl of preparation for the Christmas celebration with my family, but to my dismay, with each passing day, my body once again began to develop symptoms, and I became weaker and weaker. At times, I even found it difficult to breathe. I realized that a secondary infection had probably developed in my lungs, and though I felt bad, I thought it would quickly pass. It did not. The symptoms continued to worsen.

A couple of the symptoms that I began to notice were an incessant cough, most certainly caused by pneumonia that had developed, and a strange crackling sound coming from my lungs when I would take a breath. I had never experienced that before, so it was a bit concerning, but still, I continued on with my tasks.

One evening, after returning from being out and about running errands, the crackling sounds were no longer happening just when I would take a breath, it became continuous, even between breaths. I suddenly became extremely weak. Assuming that the weakness was due to needing something to eat, I fixed a sandwich and sat down in the recliner to eat it. With each bite I would take, I began to realize that I could hardly swallow. My throat wasn't sore at all, but it felt as though something was blocking my esophagus, and restricting the food from going down.

Then my body suddenly started to swell. My clothes felt so tight! I loosened my belt and unfastened my jeans, but even then, it felt as though something was squeezing me very tightly. Then I could hardly breathe at all.

Though difficult, I somehow made my way to the bedroom and lay down on the bed. I wasn't completely sure what was happening, but I knew and could feel that something was seriously wrong. In just a matter of minutes,

I had been thrown into what felt like a battle for my life. It was as if the air I breathed in was being trapped in my chest cavity.

I lifted my hands toward Heaven, and I began to pray. I could feel fear trying to grip my mind. I immediately began to take authority over that fear, refusing to come into agreement with the thoughts the enemy was trying to convince me to believe. I turned my focus onto the Lord and prayed, "Jesus, You see what is happening with me. You are all-wise, and You know all things. I need You to help me. I don't know what this is, but You do. I don't know what to do, but You do. I am asking You to give me wisdom. Show me what to do. If I need to go to the hospital, I will go, but if You want to heal me now, I will trust You. I just need wisdom. Help me, Lord!"

As that prayer left my lips, I heard the Lord say to me, "You can trust Me. It won't be easy, but if You will listen and obey Me, you will experience a miracle tonight."

I felt that I had entered the arena of a spiritual fight. At the same time, I also felt grace—the divine influence of Heaven—enter that room to help me in this time of need (see Hebrews 4:16).

Then a thought immediately came into my spirit. It wasn't my own thought. I knew it was wisdom from the Lord. "Get your phone and search for information about the lungs."

I did that, and the site that I found gave information about each part of the lungs and their function. I then felt the Lord say, "With that information, begin to command, with confidence and authority, each part of your lungs to function the way I created them to function!"

In 1 Corinthians 9:27, Paul reveals that we have the authority to "discipline and bring our bodies under subjection." That phrase means that, like an athlete, we can discipline our bodies, bringing them under subjection or submission to God so that they do what they are supposed to do.

So, using the information on the website and the instruction in the Word of God, in the authority of Jesus and the Word, I began to call each part of my lungs by name and commanded them to do their work.

I knew it was not by my might or power that I would overcome this spirit of infirmity that was seeking to destroy me. There was nothing that I could have done on my own to change the situation. I became fully reliant on Holy Spirit to enable me to be victorious in this battle. I could feel Him working with me to forbid and deny my lungs to come under subjection to any influence that was trying to oppose the healing power of the Lord Jesus. He empowered me to speak to my lungs by faith, and I commanded them to function the way that God had created them to function.

Following is a basic recount of my declarations:

Lungs, I command you to come under subjection to the authority of Jesus Christ. I do not give you permission to submit to any other influence. You will function the way God created you to function. You will make oxygen available to my body, and you will remove the other gasses from my body. When I inhale the air through my nose or mouth, that air will travel down my pharynx, pass through my larynx and into my trachea. Nothing will obstruct or hinder this process. Bronchial tubes, you will function the way you are made to function. Alvcoli, you tiny air sacs at the end of the bronchial tubes, you will do your work to transfer the oxygen from the inhaled air into my blood. You will not burst or malfunction. The blood will then carry oxygen into my heart, and heart, you will pump that oxygenated blood through my body, and the cells of my tissues and organs will receive it the way they were created to receive it. I forbid bronchitis, pneumonia, or any form of respiratory infection, lung injury, or disorder to hinder this process. By faith in Jesus Christ and in His name and authority, I command you to do what you were created to do! No other power shall handle me, but the power of the living God! No other spirit shall have influence over me, but the Spirit of the living God! Amen!

Again, these words were not my own! I opened my mouth, and Holy Spirit filled it with the Father's words as

I reviewed the anatomy and physiology of the lungs. As He had said to me earlier that evening, it wasn't easy. I had to continue to bring my thoughts under subjection to the authority of Jesus and the Word of God. I had to continuously cast down fear as the Lord gave me grace to stand and to keep standing.

Through my willingness to submit my entire body to the Lord in that moment, it was as if Holy Spirit completely overtook my thoughts, my mouth, and my situation. He prayed for me when I didn't know what to pray. He worked through me in ways I never would have thought to work. It was a true demonstration and activation of the words declared in Romans 8:26-27 (AMP): "...the Spirit [comes to us and] helps us in our weakness. We do not know what prayer to offer or how to offer it as we should, but the Spirit Himself [knows our need and at the right time] intercedes on our behalf with sighs and groanings too deep for words. And He who searches the hearts knows what the mind of the Spirit is because the Spirit intercedes [before God] on behalf of God's people in accordance with God's will."

I could feel the swirl of warfare, but I knew the Lord was with me, fighting for me as I came into agreement with Him and with His Word. It was an extremely intense time, but years of experience had taught me that Jesus is my Great Physician and God is Jehovah Rapha. Step by step, He instructed me, and I obeyed.

I wasn't in denial of the symptoms that I was still feeling at work in my body, but in child-like faith, I was laying hold of and wielding the Sword of the Spirit, which is the Word of God.

This battle lasted several hours, but little by little, I began to feel those symptoms leave. The crackling sounds stopped, the swelling in my body decreased, strength began to return, and my breathing became easy and normal again.

Holy Spirit helped, instructed, and comforted me in my time of need, and Jesus healed me completely! The next morning, I awoke to find that my body was whole. It was as though that infirmity had never even been there!

While this was a physical attack on my body, it was also a spiritual attack. We have a very real adversary, and it is his mission to kill, steal, and destroy. His modus operandi has always been to bring suggestions to play on our emotions in an attempt to get us to come into agreement with him. Our agreement then gives him permission to work his plan against us. This is why the Word informs us that though we walk in the flesh, we do not war according to the flesh. For the weapons of our warfare are not carnal but mighty in God for pulling down strongholds. We are then instructed to cast down arguments and every high thing that exalts itself against the knowledge of God, bringing every thought into captivity to the obedience of Christ (see 2 Corinthians 10:3-5).

Everyone's experiences are not the same, so we have to search out what the will of God is for each situation we may face and seek His wisdom and instruction for what to do. When we know His will and instruction, we must bring our thoughts and our bodies under subjection to His authority. We must speak His Word and obey His instructions with confidence that He will be with us, and He will work through us His wonders to perform, for our good and for His glory!

The Power We've Been Given

The Lord gave me two dreams in which I saw and became a recipient of what was referred to as a "mantle of revival." I wrote at length about both of these dreams in my book, *Carry On.*[3] That mantle represented the spiritual inheritance that we have received as heirs of God and joint heirs with Jesus. It is a powerful and power-filled inheritance. This "mantle" did not come from a man; it came from Jesus Himself, and it manifested to the Church on the day of Pentecost, as recorded in Acts chapter two.

In the second of the two dreams, some friends and I had just completed a prayer assignment, and we were asking the Lord, "What do we do now?" As we sat together, waiting to hear a response, a car pulled into the parking lot in front of us. An elderly lady emerged from the vehicle. She was bent over and emaciated, just skin and bones. She was having a very difficult time getting out of the car, so in this dream, I saw myself run over to help her. She thanked me for helping her, and I then invited her to come and sit with us. I led her to the picnic table where my friends and I were sitting. Though in the dream I knew it was a hot summer day, the lady was dressed as though it was winter. I asked her if she was cold, and she said that she was. I then said to her, "Well, we have this mantle. I told her the mantle was too heavy and too big to put the whole thing on her, but we could wrap the corner of it around her. My friends and I did just that, and instantly, the woman was made completely whole! Right before our eyes, her body filled out, she stood up straight, completely restored!

As the dream continued, there were others who came and stood before us with various health, mental, and spiritual needs, and one by one, we would wrap the corner of that mantle around them and they were instantly healed, delivered, and made whole. My friends and I were rejoicing with each person, and we were all in complete awe of what was happening.

In the dream, the Lord spoke audibly, my friends and I all heard Him. He said, "I gave you the mantle of revive-all. It is to revive. It is to make alive again. It is to bring change. It is not for looks, and it's not for the exaltation of those who wear it. It is not to be worn and just talked about for its beauty and power. There is purpose for the mantle, and there is purpose for My putting the mantle on you. Now, I Am going to teach you how to use it for My intended purposes. This is My answer to your question,

'What do we do now?' Now, you must learn how to use the mantle."

The two dreams have deeply impacted my life. They depict profound revelation and illustration of God's intentions for the Body of Christ. Acceptance of Jesus as our Savior and Lord is not just about getting us to Heaven, it's about connecting us to God and the power to fulfill the purposes for which we were created. We are not here on this earth just to bide our time until Jesus returns. We are heirs of His powerful inheritance, and as His heirs, He sends us forth to be His representatives, His witnesses. He instructs us to be filled with His Spirit, Who enables us to carry on with the things that He began to do and to teach. We are to shine as lights in this dark world, impacting others with the reality of our resurrected Savior, Who still gives hope, healing, life, and peace.

We are in Christ, and He is in us. He has given us His Spirit, clothed us in His righteousness. We have an inheritance of power, and He says to us, "There is purpose for the mantle (spiritual inheritance), and there is purpose for My putting the mantle on you. Now, I Am going to teach you how to use it for My intended purposes. Now, you must learn how to use the mantle."

A few months after I had the first "revival mantle" dream, a friend of mine presented me with a beautiful quilt that she had made for me. She had made a few quilts and had presented them to various people, as the Lord instructed her to do so. Each quilt is very prophetic, in that each piece means something spiritual to the recipient. The quilt she gave to me is very large, and I was deeply moved by her willingness to make and give to me such a beautiful, extravagant, and meaningful gift.

When she makes the quilts, the Lord gives her a name for each one. The name He instructed her to call mine was, "The Revival Mantle." Amazing!

Then a few months after having the second dream, my friend came to me and said, "I made another quilt for you!" I was just taken aback and overwhelmed! She told me she made it from the remnants of the first quilt she had made for me and that it was a smaller version of the larger quilt. She had thought that I would be able to more easily carry the smaller quilt with me since the other one was so "big and heavy."

Since that time, I have taken that smaller quilt with me on several prayer assignments, including to the location near Murphy, North Carolina that was highlighted in both dreams.

Then, in the fall of 2024, I was scheduled to minister in northern Indiana. The Lord had not given me full instruction as to what I would be preaching about in the meeting. All He had said was that He wanted me to speak about the revival mantle dreams. Just before I left my home that morning, I heard the Lord say to me, "Take that smaller quilt with you." I had no idea why He was instructing me to take it, but I went to my bedroom and got the quilt from the closet. As I was placing it into my suitcase, the Lord asked me a question. "Do you know what that is?" My brilliant answer was, "Umm, it's a quilt." I guess I thought He didn't know that and I probably had to inform Him.

His reply was so powerful and deeply impacting. "It's a representation of the corner of the mantle, and it's time to start using it!"

The Lord instructed me to take that quilt to the meeting there in Indiana. At the end of the message, everyone came forward, and the Lord then led me to lay it on every person, one by one, and pray for them. During that time, many were touched by the Lord in a powerful way, and some received instant healing in their bodies.

There is nothing special about the quilt, except that, for me, it is a special treasure. But like the handkerchiefs and parts of Paul's clothing that we read about in Acts 19:12, God does sometimes use material things as a point of contact in order to manifest His healing. There is power in what these things represent. They represent the desire of God to touch people. They represent His power to change what needs to be changed, heal what needs to be healed, and deliver those who will receive His deliverance. They represent the authority and inheritance Jesus has given to us as His joint-heirs. You may not have a special quilt or a handkerchief or prayer cloth to use when you pray, and that's okay. What we all, as born-again believers in Christ, do have is access to His power that came from

Him to us by the Spirit, and now, He is saying, "It's time to start using it."

The power is real, and it is available to all who receive Him as Savior and believe His Word. Jesus said, "Most assuredly, I say to you, he who believes in Me, the works that I do he will do also; and greater works than these he will do, because I go to My Father" (John 14:12 NKJV). I believe we are now in the time when Jesus is restoring His Body to operate in the fullness of His intentions. Jesus is still the Miracle Worker, and our God is still Jehovah Rapha, the Lord our Healer. In this redemptive movement that we have entered into, there are those who will rise with revelation of what we have received, and we will operate with the evidence of His power as He works in us and through us to make Himself known. It's time to know about and to use the "mantle" of our spiritual inheritance!

8

Paths

The steps of a [good and righteous] man are directed and established by the Lord, and He delights in his way [and blesses his path].

—Psalm 37:23 AMP

I have always been intrigued with pathways. As a photographer, I love to take pictures of paths that are meandering through the woods. The allure to follow and discover where the path is leading calls to me somehow.

I've walked down many a path to find that the journey itself was the discovery. Other paths I've hiked led to cabins once inhabited by pioneers from long ago. Still, others led to open meadows with views that would nearly take your breath away. All of these things would be left undiscovered if I had chosen to ignore the paths. It may not always be easy, but in order to experience the wonders of what lies before us, we must determine that the rewards of discovery are greater than the momentary sacrifice of personal comfort.

Sometimes pathways have yet to be formed and must be made. Some are well-trodden and can be easily followed. Others are there but are barely seen. After years of no one traveling on it, a path becomes overgrown and hidden under brush and trees and such, and its purpose is forgotten or abandoned. But when someone rediscovers the path and begins to clear away the overgrowth, its purpose can be reclaimed.

We are each on a journey to make, find, and follow the paths to which God has called us. These are ancient paths that have been known and marked by God from the foundation of the world, just waiting for us to enter our time on the timeline. He knows the plans that He has for us (see Jeremiah 29:11), and as we cooperate with Him, following His leading, we can step into the wonder and abundance of His intended purposes. To follow His path is to discover the treasures He has for us, making life far more meaningful and exciting.

The Lord, by His Spirit, will guide us, and I have found that following Him is the ultimate great adventure! It has always been my prayer that I would be a discoverer and follower of the path that He has marked for me. I also desire that He would grant to me the wisdom to uncover any path that has been lost or abandoned in previous generations that still holds necessary purposes for our time. If we choose to know and obey His desires, then we will become influencers and initiators. Old waste places will be rebuilt, the foundations of many generations will be raised up, breaches will be repaired, and paths in which to dwell will be restored. When we are willing to follow His leading, He will give us wisdom, favor, and the ability to reclaim and restore the purposes and direction that He has always intended (see Isaiah 58:12).

Some choose to settle and never walk the path that was intended for them, leaving experiences unclaimed and making the journey more difficult for the next generation. But there are others who choose to go beyond the boundaries of what is comfortable and familiar and explore the fullness of the journey that God has designed for them. Their faith walk becomes a testimony of experiences with Him that leaves a path for future generations to discover, thereby provoking them to want to know and take the journey that has been mapped out for their lives in their time.

The Bible says that God will "show us the path of life" (see Psalm 16:11). He will order our steps. If we choose to follow Him, the path will become more than a speculation; it will become a journey of revelation and discovery of His ways, wonders, and purposes that are so much greater than our human minds could even think to imagine. The longer we follow His leading, the more He will reveal to us. The "more" that He has in store will only be discovered as we take the journey with Him, humbling ourselves to walk with Him, and trusting Him to order and direct our steps.

The Right Place at the Right Time

Our journey is not measured in years, it's measured in steps. To take the steps is to discover the purposes of God for our journey. What each step has to reveal will only be discovered and experienced as we choose to trust God and obediently follow Him as He leads us along the path that He has charted for our lives.

While God does see the end from the beginning and He already knows the plans that He has for our lives, the truth is, that He doesn't show us the whole picture. Sometimes He just shows us a step. Sometimes He creates an opportunity. Sometimes He gives us an idea. But if we fail to take the step, seize the opportunity, or explore the idea, then we will never see the full picture of what could have been. It's like the old saying, "If we ask God for an oak tree, He gives us an acorn. What we do with the acorn determines whether or not we ever see the oak tree!"

The revealing of the big picture of God's purposes comes as we obey His leading and follow His chosen path. Sometimes those acts of obedience will take us out of our comfort zones or require of us more than we think that we can do or give. This is why we must develop a strong relationship with the Lord and keep our focus on Him and not on ourselves. If we look to ourselves, our resources, our knowledge, our limited abilities, then we will fail to believe God beyond those resources, knowledge, and limitations because His leading will, more often than not, take us beyond what we can achieve on our own.

Dependency on God is a must when choosing to devote ourselves to Him. That dependency is developed by relationship with Him: spending time with Him, reading the Bible, praying in the Spirit, worshiping Him. The more time we devote to Him, the more we know Him. The more we know Him, the more we will trust Him. The more we trust Him, the more we will obey Him. The more we obey Him, the more we experience His faithfulness and the more our trust and dependency in Him is solidified.

Sometimes, we don't even realize that our steps are being ordered. We're just living our lives, but as we devote ourselves to the Lord, we can trust that He always sees what we don't yet see and that He knows what we don't yet know. We plan our way, but He orders our steps.

Necessary Steps

A few years ago, my friend, Darlene, and I decided to take an early morning walk in Cades Cove in the Great Smoky Mountains National Park and take some pictures. The cool morning air meeting with the warmth of the rising sun, had created a foggy blanket that settled in the fields, leaving us with amazing opportunities to capture some of God's highlighted beauty in creation.

One of the most captivating scenes was found when we came to a gate next to a stream. Beyond the gate lay a wide, open field with only a lone tree standing in its center. The fog had wrapped itself around the tree, creating an artistic masterpiece of beauty that nearly took my breath away! Laying all of our extra gear aside, we freed ourselves to begin snapping the photos of this picturesque scene.

After some time, we decided we must move on in order to discover more things to photograph. Eventually, we arrived back at our vehicle and decided to then take a drive through the Cove. Just as we entered the car, Darlene realized that she had lost her glasses. A diligent search through her things came up empty, so, our only choice was to retrace our steps from the morning's walk. With the day wearing on, we decided to drive the loop to search for the lost glasses.

Stopping at every location we could recall where we had been taking photos earlier in the morning, our search still turned up empty. Darlene then made a faith statement, declaring, "God wants to help me with this. He sees where my glasses are, and He will show me where to find them!"

At that moment, we remembered the gate. We had stayed there for a while, and Darlene recalled that during our time there, she had taken her glasses off and tucked them into her shirt pocket. After that, she had climbed through the fence in order to get a better view of the field. Maybe the glasses had fallen out of her pocket.

We made our way back to the scene, and sure enough, to her relief, there on the ground in the tall grass next to the fence, lay her glasses.

The time it had taken us to retrace our steps to find the glasses had delayed us a bit that day, but we were not deterred. We were determined to still take our time and enjoy the journey.

That drive around the loop road is normally peaceful and inviting, but one of my tires had picked up a small pebble along the way, and the clicking sound was severely invading my peace, so I stopped to remove it. As I got down beside the tire to remove the gravel, a group of young people whizzed by me on bicycles. They seemed excited and in a hurry. I got back into the car and we continued on, eventually passing the enthusiastic cyclists. However, several of them soon picked up their pace and rode on ahead of us out of sight.

The one-way road through Cades Cove is narrow and curvy, and at times, leads down some pretty steep hills. We had arrived at one of those hills and were just making our way down it when one of the young cyclists went past us at a very high rate of speed. She was obviously trying to catch up with the rest of the group. We instantly could see that the steep incline had taken her by surprise, and she had lost control of her bike. She was rapidly and violently shaking her handlebars back and forth and was quickly gaining speed. She didn't seem to be able to apply the brakes, and at the bottom of the hill, she collided with the rear of a parked SUV. She struck the vehicle so hard the glass in the liftgate was broken and the bumper was dented.

The collision left her injured and temporarily unconscious.

Darlene had worked in the medical field for many years, so her immediate thought was to stop to see if there was anything we could do to help the young girl. We ran to find her now lying on the ground, beside her badly damaged bicycle. Darlene did a quick assessment of the obvious injuries that the girl had sustained, and it was almost certain that she had some type of injury to her head. Her eyes were beginning to swell from the face-first impact. There were also several cuts and scrapes on her hands and legs, one of which was a deep gash on her knee where she had hit it on the vehicle's trailer hitch.

Darlene made sure that the girl's neck was kept in alignment, while I applied ointment and bandages to the cuts and scrapes. With only a simple first-aid kit, there really wasn't a lot that we could do, but we did all that we could.

As the girl began to regain awareness, Darlene asked her several questions: "What's your name? Do you know where you are? Where are you hurting? Do you know what day of the week this is?" Thankfully, she seemed to remember things correctly, and no bones seemed to be broken, but the girl was really scared, and she was crying. Darlene was talking to her in an effort to get her to relax. Eventually, the conversation turned toward the Lord, and there was an undeniable peace that suddenly came over the whole scene. The young lady became very calm as

Darlene prayed with her and for her. Within minutes, she became very alert, and soon a National Park ranger arrived and transported her to a local hospital for further assessment and observation.

At the end of that day, Darlene and I retraced our steps in our minds, and the more we thought and talked about it, the more we concluded that God had orchestrated our whole day's journey. He led us to make the decision to take that early morning photography walk. And every step we took was necessary to position us in that exact moment so that He could work through us to bring help and comfort to that young girl in her desperate time of great need. What a great and loving God!

Even when our journey seemed to be delayed by our unexpected search for Darlene's lost glasses or when the gravel in the tire interrupted my peace, prompting me to stop and remove it, those steps were necessary for God's purpose being fulfilled.

It's an amazing thing to be in the right place at the right time. Even more amazing is the realization that God orders our steps to position us in the right place at the right time. Even though we are more often than not unaware of the importance of the steps on our journey, still every step matters, especially when we make the choice to follow God's path for our lives. Even in what seems to be insignificant detours, God directs us so that He can position us to work through us to make Christ known.

Purpose in the Journey

As I look back over my life's journey, I can retrace my steps and see how involved God has been in directing them. It's quite amazing to realize that He charted my course and that He has been there navigating my steps all along the way. It's true for us all. Every part of the journey has been connected to another part that was connected to another part. Step by step, the Lord has been leading us. When we take the time to look back, we will see the amazing tapestry that God has been weaving all along our path and how each part was so important to getting us to where we are and for molding us into who we are today.

There's purpose in the journey. Strewn along our path are important things waiting for us to discover, experience, and do. In His set time, the Lord will direct us right to those things for His purposes to be realized and accomplished. So, just keep walking and don't let the delays and detours concern you. Sometimes, it's not actually a delay or a detour. Sometimes God is just keeping you in step with His plan to get you to the right place at the right time.

David's prayer in Psalm 25:4 was, "Show me Your ways, O LORD; Teach me Your paths" (KJV). This prayer should become our prayer. We are each here for only a moment in time, and it passes so quickly. May we choose to live our "moment" for Christ and His purposes. May we stay the course, follow His path, and leave nothing undone that we ought to do!

A Capable Guide

For each of our lives, the Lord has gone before us and charted a course for us to take. It's the path of purpose that He has chosen for us. He doesn't expect us to figure out the way on our own. Sometimes, the path may be clearly seen; at other times, it may require faith with no sight. Regardless of how the path forward is presented, we must choose to allow our trust in the Lord to provoke our steps. He knows the way. He is the Way, and He has given us Holy Spirit as our Guide. There is nothing about our journey that He doesn't know. While we may not yet be able to see and know everything about the path ahead, Holy Spirit is constantly searching out the deep things in the mind of God, and He will show those things to us in various ways and by different means in order to make known to us His thoughts concerning us (see 1 Corinthians 2:9-12). We can confidently follow His directions as He keeps us on track with God's course for our lives. He will never mislead us or bring us out in the wrong place, as long as we stay in step with His guidance.

Sometimes we may not even realize our steps are being ordered. But there are other times when we will know that the Lord is instructing us to do certain things. We may not fully understand the purpose of His leading, but we must be obedient to His leading. That obedience will unlock God's purpose. And it must be understood that we may never even know the full purpose of why He leads us to do the things He instructs us to do. Our focus is not on the path, and our obedience is not contingent upon understanding the outcome. Our focus is on our Guide, and our obedience is given because we love Him and we trust Him.

The path of God's intentions for us will often lead us to moments or situations that require us to take leaps of faith. The courage to take those leaps of faith is developed by our growing knowledge of the Word of God and by the demonstrations of the power of God that we experience as we walk with Him along the way. He allows us to go through moments and experiences that teach us more and more about who He is and what He can do. The more we know about Him, the less we will lean on our own understanding and the stronger our faith in Him becomes.

As the saying goes, "hindsight is 20/20." As I have been writing this book, I have reflected on so many memories of things I have witnessed, heard, and done through the years. At the time, I didn't have a full perspective of what was happening. I was mostly just living my life. But now, looking back, I clearly see that God was working through those experiences to teach me about Himself. Those moments when He protected me, provided for me, healed me, introduced me to the right people, and positioned me in the right places at the right times were not just momentary happenings; they were key moments in which He was equipping and positioning me for what was ahead. Those amazing revelations and experiences have become reference points to give me assurance and a confident knowing that He is with me and that He is able and willing to take care of me. That knowing has been a great comfort to me as I have taken this journey down the path of purpose that He has chosen for my life.

So often we are guilty of taking things for granted. If we are not careful, we will surely overlook the very things, people, or circumstances that God places in our lives to help us get from where we are to where He is taking us. He knows exactly what is needed to steer us in the direction of His plans and purposes for our lives, and if we will pay attention, He will mark and clear the way for our successful navigation.

I have always loved Proverbs 3:5-6: "Trust in and rely confidently on the Lord with all your heart and do not rely on your own insight or understanding. In all your ways know and acknowledge and recognize Him, and He will make your paths straight and smooth [removing obstacles that block your way]" (AMP). The focus of this proverb is not so much on straight and smooth paths, but rather on the fact that if we will devotedly follow and focus on the Lord, He will clear our paths of hindering obstacles so that we can successfully walk with Him. He sees the end from the beginning, and He has charted our course. The journey is ours for the taking, but the fulfillment of God's intentions for our lives along the journey will only be fully realized as we trust in, rely on, recognize, and acknowledge the Lord in all of our ways. By faith in Him, we can follow the path and discover all the journey has in store.

9

Guidance

Show me Your ways, O Lord; Teach me Your paths. Lead me in Your truth and teach me, for You are the God of my salvation; On You I wait all the day.

–Psalm 25:4, 5 NKJV

At a young age, God began to give me revelation and understanding, showing me that He was ordering my steps, and this caused me to genuinely begin to go deeper in my relationship with Christ. I longed to know and to hear Him and to be guided by His Spirit. It was only a matter of time before He led me to the first of many leaps of faith that I would be confronted with throughout my journey.

I distinctly remember a moment in my life when I had come to the place where I felt I had done all that I could do with what I had known and received up to that time. I had a deep knowing that there was more that God had for me, but I was overwhelmed with a feeling of uncertainty of how to advance. I shared my feelings with a very seasoned older saint who imparted to me great wisdom that has stuck with me since that time. She said, "When your journey brings you to a place that requires you to move beyond your current wisdom and experiences, you must stop, get away with the Lord, fast, and pray in the Spirit until you feel the charge of God's anointing, wisdom, and revelation moving you on to the next chapter of what He has waiting for you."

I did just that. For three days, I shut myself off from the world, fasted, and prayed in the Spirit. During that time, the Lord gave to me a vision in which I saw what appeared to be a movie playing on the wall of my room. Faces. Hundreds of faces were flashing before me one after the other: Asian faces, African faces, Native American faces, Hispanic faces, European faces. This continued for several minutes, and then I heard the Lord say, "I am sending you to the nations." Though this wasn't a new instruction, it was a moment that forever changed my life. I knew without doubt that this was the time of fulfillment for things He had spoken and shown to me even in my youth. He never forgets His promises, and He always knows and remembers the plans that He has woven over our lives.

In the fourth chapter of the book of Revelation, the voice of the Lord called to John saying, "Ascend and enter. I'll show you what happens next" (Revelation 4:1 MSG). Sometimes we just have to stop and listen so that we can hear from a higher perspective and gain necessary and timely insight that will help us to align with the Lord as He navigates us according to the path He has charted. Though I didn't receive clear understanding of how my journey would unfold in the days and years to come, I was now armed with revelation of what was coming next for me.

Come and Follow Me

During that time, God developed a deep longing in my spirit to go on a mission trip. That was something I had never done before, but my heart began to burn for the nations.

There were several ways that God began to confirm this calling. One of these confirmations came through a book that was given to me by my cousin. The book was based on the life of a young lady who felt the call of God to go and live in the remote Appalachian Mountains to teach in a mission school in the early 1900s. She had never lived away from her home, and she had never known the woes of poverty, yet she was willing to follow the Lord's leading for her life. As the story unfolds, one can easily detect how the hand of the Lord was upon her, providing for her needs and guiding her every step. This was a very serious and bold move on the part of this young lady. It was a different time then. There were no telephones, no convenience stores on every corner, no restaurants. She would be living in a very remote mountain community where she knew no one, and the culture and ways of those among whom she would be living were completely foreign to her. I'm sure fear was a temptation for her, but the call of God was stronger than the nudge of fear, and she obeyed.

This woman lived many years before I was even born, and yet her story deeply impacted my life. It wasn't a coincidence that my cousin gave me that book when she did. It was a perfectly timed gift from the Lord. That lady's story gave me insight that was so beneficial to me for my own story that was beginning to unfold. Her words inspired me to look beyond myself and obey God with complete confidence and trust in His ability and faithfulness to guide me and to provide all that I would need to fulfill the call He had made known to me.

With this calling burning in my spirit, I had no idea how to even begin. I tried to connect with a group of short-term missionaries, but that didn't work out. Then, one day just out of the blue, I met a couple who was taking mission teams to various nations around the world. I shared with them the calling that I felt God was awakening inside me, and they were all excited to tell me that I could go with them on their next trip. Then, unexpectedly, at the last minute, something happened, and the trip had to be cancelled. I cannot tell you how utterly disappointed I was, yet I was equally determined to find my place! I knew God had called me, and I knew He would somehow make a way for His will to happen.

Sometimes the path may lead us to what seems to be a dead end or a delay. These times will often test our faith and seek to cause us to doubt our ability to hear God. But we must remember that our faith is in God, not in circumstances. God always speaks with intent to perform. I take great comfort in the following words written in Joshua 21:45: "Not a word failed of any good thing which the Lord had spoken...All came to pass" (NKJV).

Delays are not denials, and roadblocks are not stopping places. Everything may not happen in the way and time that we had planned, but that's not always a sign that we missed God. God has ordered the steps, and we just have to watch for the right steps and take them at the right time so that we stay in alignment with His intentions for our lives.

Later that same year, I received a telephone call from my Aunt Sadie. She was so excited to tell me about an interview she had just listened to on a local radio program. She normally didn't listen to that particular program, but "for some reason" she had decided to listen on that day! The program featured a lady who was talking about a mission team she was about to lead for a project in Central America. The lady's name was Mildred Reed. (I respectfully refer to her as Sister Reed.) Sister Reed had actually been scheduled to be on that radio program several months prior, but due to an ice storm, the interview had to be rescheduled. The day my aunt "just happened" to be listening was the rescheduled date. If the original date had been kept, Sadie would not have been tuned in. God had orchestrated the unfolding of the next part of my journey! He had it planned all along. Imagine that!

On the radio program, Sister Reed talked about her daughter and son-in-law, Linda and Earl Yielding, who were, at that time, serving as directors of a school in a remote part of Belize, Central America. As Sister Reed was speaking on the program, my aunt realized that she knew the daughter and son-in-law of whom she spoke. Sadie and my Uncle Ernest had been friends with Earl and Linda many years before!

Before God even awakened the calling in me, He had already been putting pieces in place so that at the right time, He could connect those pieces to form a clear picture that would validate His leading. Amazing!

At the end of the radio interview, Sadie jotted down the phone number and told me to give this woman a call. When I spoke with Sister Reed on the telephone, she told me that the trip was scheduled for the following summer, but the set number of team members she was prepared to take with her had already been filled, and there wasn't really room for any more. However, she was meeting with the team members in her home that following week to make preparations for the upcoming trip, and she invited me to come and sit in at that meeting.

I didn't go to the meeting alone. Several of my family members joined me. One by one we walked through the door as Brother and Sister Reed greeted each of us. Having never met these people before, everyone was introducing themselves, saying their names as they shook hands with our hosts. I reached out my hand, but before I could say a word, Sister Reed said, “You are Gina, and God told me to take you on this trip.” Six months later, I was on my first mission trip. My heart was running over with joy and excitement! This would prove to be a major step on my life’s journey.

Once we landed in Belize, we gathered all of our luggage and supplies and were then driven to the school where we would be staying for the next couple of weeks. The first night we were there, our team met with the missionaries who were working at the school. We were discussing our agenda for the next two weeks. Suddenly, I felt that every voice in the room went silent, and all I could hear was that still, small voice of the Lord. “I Am calling you to this land. This will be your home for a short while. I have need of you here.”

I just went kind of numb all over. One of the missionaries must have noticed that something was happening to me, and she patted my knee and asked if I was okay. I knew I was okay physically, but I also understood, at least in part, that my whole life was about to change, and I wasn’t sure that I was okay with that! I would like to tell you that I rejoiced in the news of God’s revealed plan for my life, but that’s not what happened. I quickly objected to this, trying to reason with the Lord in my mind by saying something to the effect of, “I will become a financial partner with some of the missionaries here. I will sow into them and thus be a part of what You are doing here." That was unwise because that wasn't at all what God said that I would do!

One thing I have come to understand in walking this journey with the Lord is that arguing my point with Him is about as useful as a wagon with no wheels! God sees the end from the beginning. That means that He has our lives planned out! It really is an exciting journey if we will learn to trust Him and obey His leading. We used to sing these words of an old chorus: *"Trust and obey, for there's no other way to be happy in Jesus, but to trust and obey"* (John H. Sammis, "Trust and Obey," chorus, 1887).

For several days, we worked hard and long on the projects we had gone there to do. This was a welcomed distraction for me. Then, the day before we were to fly back home from our short-term trip, our team decided to take a day of rest and relaxation. Some of the missionaries took us to an area where local artists offer their hand-made products for sale to tourists. It had been a great day until we were strolling along, slowly making our way back to the van. I was walking alone, when suddenly Earl and Linda caught up with me and struck up a conversation. In the course of that conversation, the relaxation of the moment suddenly flew away like a leaf caught in the wind.

"You know Gina, we could really use you here. We need teachers, and we think you would be a great addition to our staff. We just want you to pray and think about it."

There it was...a definite leap of faith moment, and I felt no courage at all! As a matter of fact, I felt as though my knees would buckle beneath me. I had told no one what I had heard from the Lord on our first night there, but here He was, setting it all into motion. I would love to tell you that I made my decision to obey the Lord with confidence and boldness, but the truth is, I did it afraid!

I was very young, and I had never been away from home for long periods of time, much less lived in a foreign country, but God was connecting the dots—dots that He had marked out for me even years ago. He had steered me to the exact right place and to the exact right people at the exact right time. The door was opening, and I knew I had to go through it.

This was a major step on my journey. It was a scary time, yet it turned out to be one of the most exciting and memorable times of my life. Just as He had said, that school was my "home for a short while." For seven months I lived there, and I learned many things about the Lord as I encountered Him as Provider, Protector, and faithful Father. I also learned a lot about myself. My time there prepared me for the future that was unfolding. Those valuable lessons have stayed with me throughout all of these years.

"Come, follow Me," Jesus says, "and I will send you out" (see Matthew 4:19 NIV). He's got great things in store for all of us who are willing to yield our lives to Him. He's been planning the course all along, and all He asks is that we give Him our devoted "Yes!" and obedience...even if we have to do it afraid.

10

A Right Time Door

There is a season (a time appointed) for everything and a time for every delight and event or purpose under Heaven –

–Ecclesiastes 3:1 AMP

Another key moment in my life occurred when my pastor (at that time) and his wife, Pastors Ron and Donna Smith, asked if I would come by the church office and meet with them. I agreed to do so, and we set up a date and time. On the set date, I walked into the office, not knowing what they wanted to discuss. I don't think any of us realized the true importance of that meeting, but I would later come to understand that this was a very pivotal time for me and that God's hand was being extended to direct me down a path that I otherwise would never have even seen, much less have taken.

My pastors had received an invitation to attend a mission conference in Nashville, Tennessee, and they were asked to bring one or two more people with them, if possible. After praying about it, they strongly felt that I should attend that conference. I really wasn't interested in the invitation at all. I had assumed it would just be another boring "church thing." I shared this feeling with them, meaning no disrespect, but I just wasn't interested. Pastor Smith wasn't taking no for an answer because he knew he had heard from the Lord. He said, "I feel strongly that you are supposed to be at this conference." So, reluctantly, I agreed to go. All the hotel expenses were paid for all of the attendees of that conference to stay at the beautiful Opryland Hotel, so if nothing else, it would be a refreshing and relaxing time away.

One of the requirements for attending the conference was that we must each choose and register for two breakout sessions. I was given a list of classes that I could choose from. There were only two subjects on the list that sparked any interest in me, at all. One subject was Men and Women of Action and the other was People for Care and Learning. I checked the two boxes and filled out my registration, committing myself to attend the conference.

We arrived at the hotel to find that thousands of people had come for the weekend conference. It turned out that it wasn't boring at all. It was an amazing and educational time. I learned so much about various ministries all around the world that were working in both spiritual and practical ways to show the love of Christ and to make Him known.

I found that the classes I had chosen to attend were not subject titles but were actually the names of two organizations that were involved in sending people to various parts of the world to assist in educational and evangelistic purposes, as well as disaster and humanitarian relief projects. My heart was instantly connected as I listened to each speaker's words about their outreaches.

The same unction of Holy Spirit that I had felt when the Lord called me to the mission field those years before was stirring in me again. This was another step on my journey, and for the next sixteen years, I continued to walk that path, joining and working with teams who were a part of the very organizations that I had learned about in those classes.

During those years, I experienced God's supernatural provision that enabled me to join teams in building houses and churches and taking gifts and supplies to children and local churches in some very remote parts of the world, as well as to locations throughout the Appalachian Mountain regions here in the United States of America. We assisted in several recovery and relief efforts in areas that had been devastated by tornados, tsunamis, and hurricanes, both here and abroad. I was also able to encourage leaders and fellow Christians in all of these places through teaching and sharing from the Word of God. We even had opportunities to share the Gospel with many who had never heard it before.

That weekend conference in Nashville, Tennessee was so much more than a "church thing"; it was a life-changing moment that launched me through a door that I otherwise would have never known was available for me. I'm so glad to know that even when we are reluctant because of our own misguided emotions, God can still direct our hearts to follow Him, as He keeps us on course with His intended purposes for our lives.

Write the Vision

I have loved photography since I was just a young girl. Although we live in the age of digital everything, I still love the beautiful photos that are captured by the old film cameras. I suppose it's mostly nostalgia that draws me to that form. I remember two Christmases in my young years when Momma and Daddy somehow managed to buy me a camera. The first one was a Polaroid. It would instantly develop the photo for me! I loved that camera. The next camera I received was a 110 Kodak. I had to purchase the film and then mail it off to a company to have it developed. I would wait for weeks in great anticipation of the return of the photos to see what I had captured! I took pictures of everything! Once my cousin and I even posed our Barbie dolls and made pictures of them as if they were real models!

My greatest love has always been wildlife and outdoor photography. Finding and capturing those moments that only God can create brings me a lot of joy!

I also enjoy seeing photos that have been taken by other photographers. In the summer of 2008, my nephew, Josh, and I were in a quaint shop in the mountains of East Tennessee, looking through photos that had been used to create inspirational artwork. We were admiring the great talent of the photographers and the beautiful content of each piece when suddenly, I felt a powerful wave of Holy Spirit come over me. He almost took my breath away. I stepped outside the shop and asked the Lord why I felt this wave of His presence. I heard Him say so clearly, "You must do this, and you must do it now!" Then instantly, I began to see in my spirit, a clear vision of pictures of objects that looked like letters of the alphabet. I could see that each "letter" image was situated inside square blocks with solid borders and beveled edges. The "letter photo" blocks were situated side by side to form a word, and beneath the word was an inspirational phrase.

Though I had never seen anything like this, the vision was so real. I thought that maybe we had seen this exact design in the shop, so Josh and I went back inside, and after a thorough search, we realized there was nothing there that looked like what I had seen in the vision. Again, I heard the Lord say, "You must do this, and you must do it now!"

So, for the rest of our time in the mountains, Josh and I began taking pictures of everything that looked like letters. It didn't take long before we started seeing "letters" everywhere: fence posts that looked like an "I"; trees shaped like a "Y"; and wagon wheels that made a perfect "O"! On and on it went until I had captured an image for every letter in the alphabet. It was as if the Lord had opened my eyes to see letters that had been hidden in plain sight!

When I returned home, I went straight to my computer and I prayed, "Lord, You told me to do this, and You helped us to find the letters, now teach me how to make the picture You showed me in the vision."

I had no photo editing software to work with, so I made do with what I did have, and somehow, Holy Spirit guided me and enabled me to make a design. It looked exactly like the one I had seen in the vision! I outlined my "letter photos," making them into square blocks, and used them to spell the word "Trust." Beneath the word I wrote the phrase, "No matter what circumstances surround me, the one unchangeable truth is that God is with me, and He is for me. Through it all, my trust is in the Lord." I was beyond amazed when it all came together! I framed the picture and showed it to my family. They all encouraged me to make more, and I did.

The next picture I made spelled the word, "Awakening." Even back then, God was speaking to me about the move of His Spirit that would come for the salvation of this nation! For the caption beneath the word "Awakening," I wrote the phrase that had been prophetically spoken by Ms. Billye Brim earlier that year: "One thing will save America. It is an awakening to God."

I only made two of those pictures, one of which I gave to my mom. It still hangs in her house to this day. The other one became an offering that became a key that would open a very unexpected door.

In the fall of that same year, my mom, dad, and I went to a cabin, just south of Branson, Missouri, to spend a few days. This was a prayer cabin, located on the grounds of Billye Brim Ministry's headquarters on Prayer Mountain in the Ozarks. Before we left home, we decided that during our time at the cabin, we would attend the Wednesday noon prayer meeting that would be held in the chapel of the ministry's administration building. With the cost of the trip and the cabin rental, I knew that I would not have money to put in the offering, so I asked the Lord what I could give. He told me to take the other "Awakening" picture and give it as a gift to the ministry.

Wednesday came, and I carried that framed artwork with me to the prayer meeting. It was much too large to fit in the offering basket, so I held on to it until after the meeting. Waiting outside the chapel, I was holding the framed picture in my hands, asking the Lord to show me who to give it to, when suddenly someone asked, "Where did you get that?" I turned to find a man walking toward me. He took the picture from me and asked again where I got it. I said, "I made it."

Drawing others over to have a look at the artwork, this man began to ask more questions about it. He wanted to know if I took the pictures and what editing software I had used to make the design. I had never met this man, and at that time, I didn't even know his name, but I found myself telling him the entire story, from the beginning to that moment.

He asked again what editing software I used. I told him I didn't have any photo editing software but that I had used a document software to put it all together. He was shocked by that and told me there was an easier way to do it. It turned out that this man and his wife worked for Ms. Billye Brim's ministry and had a lot of experience with photography and photo editing. He invited me to meet with him and his wife the next morning and they would give me a quick tutorial of other software tools that would benefit me. He then said, "You need to do this for a living. You have definitely got an eye for it!"

I hardly slept that night. The next morning, I met with that couple, and they told me all about the latest and best photo editing software. They also gave me other information that really helped to launch me with at least a bit more confidence and assurance that this was something that I really needed to do!

I left that meeting with a mixture of excitement and a bit of disappointment. The software they said I needed was going to cost hundreds of dollars (at that time), and I had no idea how I would ever be able to get it. And even if I could get it, I had no idea how to use it. The more I tossed it around in my mind, the more I found myself being overwhelmed with disappointment and uncertainty. Then

I remembered Proverbs 3:5-6, and hope began to rise. "Trust in the Lord with all your heart, and lean not on your own understanding; in all your ways acknowledge Him, and He shall direct your paths." Though I had no idea how to move forward, I did know that God had led me that far, and I trusted that He would continue to guide my steps.

When I returned home, I began to diligently seek the Lord about this new adventure. I did not have internet access at that time—just a dial-up connection to my email—so there was no way to do any kind of research that would help me. But I decided to rely confidently on the Lord, acknowledge and recognize Him, and trust that He would remove the obstacles and show me the way forward.

The next day, I received a random email from a company that I had never even heard of. They were offering photo editing software at a deeply discounted rate for that day only! It was the exact software the couple had told me I needed, and at this discounted amount, with money that I had saved back for other needs, I had just enough to make the purchase.

One thing I learned from the email about the software was that I would need an internet connection in order to utilize certain aspects of it. I did not have an internet connection, and I didn't have the money for the monthly payment to get it, but again, I trusted that God would provide. This was a step-by-step process, and through every step, the Lord was revealing His faithfulness to me.

So, even though I didn't know how to use the software and I didn't have internet to utilize all of its capabilities, I knew this email could not have been a coincidence, so I called the number that was provided, and by faith, I made the purchase.

Just a few hours later, I received a telephone call from someone saying, "We feel the Lord wants us to start sending you a monthly offering so that you can use it to receive internet services!" Wow! God never ceases to amaze me! With that monetary assistance, I was able to sign up for an internet service.

A few weeks later, the software arrived. I was so excited! I loaded it up on my computer, and I was immediately overwhelmed. I had no idea what to do! Having never worked with such a program before, it all seemed extremely complicated. I just sat at my computer, staring at the screen.

At that exact moment, the telephone rang. I answered, and on the other end of the line came the voice of the man that I had met weeks before on Prayer Mountain–the very man who had told me about this program! "Hi, Miss Gina. I just wanted to touch base with you and tell you that when you do decide to purchase that editing software, give me a call, and I will walk you through the basic steps that you will need to get you started." *What?* Could this even be true? Yes, it was true! God was at work!

I said, "I have ordered the software, and I just received it today! I am, right now, sitting at my computer trying to figure out where to even begin!"

Without missing a beat, he said, "Great! Let's get started!" For the next hour he talked me through the basic steps that I needed to begin making my designs. By the end of that conversation, I had a good working understanding of the program! At that very moment, an unexpected business venture began for me!

There were many other amazing interventions made by the Lord that helped me to start a business that I would call, Vocal Images. My slogan was, "Images that speak to the heart." The name came to me one day while reading the scripture in Habakkuk chapter two, in which the Lord said, "Write the vision and make it plain on tablets, that he may run who reads it" (Habakkuk 2:2 NKJV). As I was reading that verse, the Lord led me to another translation in The Message Bible that says, "...Write what you see. Write it out in big block letters so that it can be read on the run." This exactly described the artwork I would be making, and it was just another undeniable confirmation to assure me that I had heard from the Lord.

"You have to do this now!" Part of the destiny of God within me had met up with the timing of God for me. I chose to take that first leap of faith, and I quickly discovered that He had miraculously orchestrated every step that was needed for the journey ahead. What had started as a vision the Lord gave to me in a photo gallery ended up being a business that would provide income to assist me in my ministry travels and livelihood for several years, until the day that I dissolved the company.

We may not always understand the leading of the Lord, but it is important to know that sometimes He speaks to us of the future that He sees unfolding in order to prepare us for what is coming next. When He speaks to us about ourselves, He's not always basing His assessment on things we have or can do in the moment in which He speaks. He speaks to the destiny that is in us and begins to breathe on that destiny to bring it forth in its preordained time. He speaks His Word, and it awakens the destiny. It also awakens us to an awareness of the destiny. In those moments, it is so important that we hear and trust His leading and obey Him quickly and completely.

That can sometimes be challenging and stretching, but He takes us from faith to faith and from glory to glory. That means He may stretch us beyond our limitations, but He will be pleased with our faith to follow Him, and He will enable us to do things that are beyond our ability, for His glory. We will receive what my friend calls, "God-ability," and operating under the influence of His ability, we will discover the miraculous revealing of His intended purposes becoming a reality in our lives.

It was no coincidence that the first picture God showed to me in the vision included the word, "Trust!"

One of my favorite old hymns comes to my mind as I write this chapter:

'Tis so sweet to trust in Jesus,
Just to take Him at His Word;
Just to rest upon His promise;
Just to know, "Thus saith the Lord."

Jesus, Jesus, how I trust Him!
How I've proved Him o'er and o'er!
Jesus, Jesus, precious Jesus!
O, for grace to trust Him more.

I'm so glad I learned to trust Thee,
Precious Jesus, Savior, Friend;
And I know that Thou art with me,
Wilt be with me to the end.

–(Louisa M. R. Stead, "'Tis So Sweet to Trust in Jesus," verse 1, chorus, and verse 4, 1882)

11

A Faith-Stretching Assignment

"Faith is deliberate confidence in the character of God whose ways you may not understand at the time."

–Oswald Chambers

A few years ago, I began to feel that familiar nudging of Holy Spirit that made me to know that I was entering a time of transition. For several days, I knew that there was something the Lord wanted me to know and to do. I often say it's like my spirit man knows something that my eyes are not yet seeing. It was that kind of feeling.

I prayed about it, and then I heard Him so clearly, in my spirit, say, "I am sending you to Texas for the entire month of September." He continued to tell me the exact location He wanted me to go, and also, He spoke about a specific church in that location that He wanted me to attend. He didn't give me exact information of all that I was to do, but He assured me that He would guide me.

This was one of those times when I knew that I had heard the Lord, but the leading was so unexpected that it made me question if I had heard Him correctly! So, for several days, I did as Mary, the mother of Jesus had done when she received specific instruction from the Lord—I silently pondered this in my heart. The longer I pondered, the stronger the nudging became. As a matter of fact, it started to feel more like a push than a nudge.

Around the third week of August, it felt like a nearly unbearable pressure was building up on the inside of me. I had not told anyone about what I had been feeling because I felt that speaking of it would be the same as committing to do it, and I just wasn't ready to do that. My daddy used to say, "Every vessel has to have a pop-off valve, or else it will explode." Well, I reached the moment when my "pop-off valve" finally reached its limit, and it opened up! Randomly throwing my arms up into the air and releasing a long stream of loud sighs was an unmistakable sign to my assistant, Darlene, that something was going on with me.

"Are you okay?"

"No! I'm not okay! God is asking me to do something that I feel I just cannot do but I know I am going to have to do!"

"What is He asking you to do?"

"He said I have to go to Texas for the entire month of September."

Making that statement out loud settled the fact that I was going to have to obey the Lord, but it also opened my eyes to an underlying fear that had somehow gone undetected by me, and it was like a living thing that was now rising up and gripping my mind and controlling my thoughts. This was an unexpected discovery. I had never really encountered this degree of fear before. I had done things and been in places where maybe I should have been afraid, but fear had never really impacted me to this degree before that moment.

Recognizing this enemy that was seeking to sabotage a critical transition in my life, I began a fast and asked God to give me understanding of what I must do to break free from the grip of fear.

A few days later, I was driving down the interstate, and suddenly the Lord showed me a quick vision in which I saw myself wielding a huge sword. In the vision, I swung that sword in a complete circle and then lifted it high over my head. Then with its point downward, I saw myself thrust the sword into the ground. I was then shown the place where the sword was now planted in the ground, and there was a word spelled out: F-E-A-R! I had thrust the sword right into the center of the word.

God said to me, "You have overcome fear. It shall have no dominion over you!"

A few days prior to this, following what I knew to be the will of the Lord had been a struggle for me, but now, exuberant expectation for the assignment was growing with every passing moment. One by one, God began dealing with every issue that had been used by the enemy to strengthen that grip of fear around me.

One amazing thing happened just three days before I set out on this journey of faith to Texas. I was in town, running some errands. I was stopped at a red light, and when the light turned green, I pressed the gas to go forward, and my vehicle would barely go. I made it through the intersection and then pulled into the parking lot of a local business where the car totally stopped and would not do anything.

I had just purchased the vehicle a few weeks prior to that day. This had been one of my hesitations in making this long trip and going to Texas alone. I had been uncertain about the integrity of the car, and now with only three days to spare before I was to leave, I had no working transportation. I barely had money to get me to Texas. I was uncertain of how I would even finance the trip, but fear had been defeated, and though the odds were being stacked against me, I now had confident faith that God was with me and that I was in His will.

I called a business owner that I had met when I purchased the vehicle. (Although not his real name, I will refer to him as Dave.) Dave's business was a used car dealership, and he had actually bought my previous car from me which enabled me to buy this vehicle from another dealership. I knew that as part of his business, he also had a wrecker service and a mechanic shop, so I contacted him to come and pick up my car. He told me it would be a while before his employee could get the wrecker to me. In the meantime, as I waited, He advised me to call the dealership where I had purchased the car and check about my warranty. When I made that call, I found out that they had misled me about the warranty and I actually had no coverage.

I shared this information with Dave when he towed my car to his shop. With the time limit I was facing, I told him the entire story of what I was doing, where I was going, and how important it was for me to leave in three days. His reply was as to be expected. "You're going to Texas and you don't know why? You don't know anybody there, and you don't have the money to even make the trip? Why would you do that?"

"Because God said to go."

"And that's enough for you? You're just going to do it?"

"Yes. God has a purpose in it, and I have to obey."

I had just enough money to get me to Texas and to pay for the first couple of nights' hotel room, so I asked Dave if he would be willing to go ahead and fix the car, and I would use the money that I had to pay him. He agreed to work with me.

A couple of days later, he called me and said, "Your car is fixed and ready to go, just come pick it up." I asked him how much it cost to fix it, and he said, "No charge! It's been taken care of!"

"What? By whom?"

He said, "You must really be following the Lord because He's working things out for you. It's the most amazing thing I've ever seen! Yesterday, I went to the auto parts store to pick up the parts for your car. I put the warranty for the parts in your name, and the guy behind the desk began to smile. I asked him what was up, and he said, "This morning before I came to work, the Lord told me to pray for Gina Gholston. I prayed that He would bless her and help her with whatever she had need of. And He brought you to my store to purchase parts for her car!" The cashier proceeded to tell Dave that he would pay for all of the parts and labor to fix the car, and if there was anything else needed, for him to come back and let him know.

Dave asked if this man at the parts store knew about my upcoming trip. The cashier and his wife are friends of mine, but at that time, I hadn't seen or talked with them for a while, and as far as I knew, they knew nothing about my trip. I just lifted my hands right there in front of Dave and began to praise the Lord for His provision!

He then said, "Well, that's not all, the man also told me to give you this envelope when you came to get your car." I opened the envelope and there was $500 inside.

Dave then began to cry right in front of me. He said, "You didn't just come here to get your car fixed. God led you here for me. I needed to be a part of this. I needed to know that God still works miracles."

For a couple of hours or so, I listened as he told me the story of a very serious situation that was happening in his life. He felt that he had no hope, but being a part of my miracle provoked him to turn to God and believe that He was working a miracle for him, as well. It was such a supernatural and humbling experience.

Before I left the shop with my vehicle, he said, "By the way, you don't have to worry about a thing with your car. I had my guys check everything and make sure the car was safe, and it's good to go."

What had felt like a setback was actually a setup for God to work, not only on my behalf but also for the man at the dealership. And the Lord also addressed one of the major concerns I had about making the trip alone, which was whether or not my car would be safe for me to drive. Now I knew! How great is our God!

As I pulled out of the parking lot, I received a text from someone I didn't really even know. A friend had given her my number, and she asked if I could meet her at her workplace. The location was just a few minutes from where I was, so, I agreed to meet with her. I arrived to find her standing outside the business, and she handed me an envelope. She said, "My mom told me what you are doing, and I just wanted to give into this assignment because I believe you are not just going there for yourself, but you are going there for us, and what you carry back will be impactful for this region."

A dear friend was with me that day, and we both just looked at each other in amazement as we knew God was working!

We left there and drove to a local department store so I could pick up some last-minute supplies. Just as we got in the car to leave, we saw a friend in the parking lot. He stopped me and said, "I want to sow an offering into this assignment you are going to do." He reached into his pocket and pulled out all the cash that he had with him and gave it to me. I was just overwhelmed.

Another of my hesitations in my obedience to do this assignment had been the fact that I knew I did not have the money. A monthlong stay would be costly, and I had hoped that during the time of keeping the leading of the Lord confidential between myself and Him would either give Him time to change His mind about the assignment or provide a windfall of funds to come to me, neither of which happened. It was a major step that would require a major leap of persuaded faith! The leap of faith had to come before the provision came! Once I made the decision to trust and obey the Lord, He then opened the windows of Heaven and began to pour out financial blessings! By the time I arrived in Texas, the whole budget for the assignment was completely filled!

The next morning, after getting my car back, I began my journey. I arrived in Texas on the last day of August and planned to leave on the first day of October so that I could be there the entire month of September.

God had provided everything that I needed. Even when I didn't understand the things that were happening around me, I look back now and know that the Lord was ordering my steps and supplying all my needs!

The day after I arrived was Sunday, and that morning I attended the church God had directed me to go to. It is a very large church, with hundreds of people attending, and I was a bit intimidated being there alone. Before entering the church, I sat in my car in the parking lot, and I said to the Lord, "I don't really know why I am here. I don't really know anyone here and no one knows me, but You know me. I am not here to be seen by man; I am here because You said to come. As long as You see me, that's all that matters."

I then began to make my way inside the church building. As I did, a lady greeted me and struck up a conversation. During the course of that conversation, she asked me where I was from. I told her, and then she asked what had brought me to the area. I told her that I was there under the instruction of Holy Spirit. I proceeded to tell her the whole story of how God told me to come and of how He had made a way for me to get there.

The lady then invited me to sit next her in the meeting. Just as the music began to play, the Apostle of the church came to the pulpit. He said, "This is very unusual because she never does this, but my wife has something she feels she needs to say before we get started."

His wife then took the microphone and said, "I feel faith in here this morning. It's not just common faith, it's something more. It's deep faith. God sees it, and I feel He wants someone in here to know that. He sees you, and He is pleased by your obedience to act on your faith."

The lady sitting next to me said, "She's talking about you!" God had confirmed to me, yet again, that His eyes were on me and that He was with me! What an added comfort that was for me.

During the course of that month, God unlocked many things inside me. He gave me deeper revelation than I had ever known about the power of working with Him in intercession. My dreams went to another level of prophetic revelation. Understanding my calling as a prophetic minister also became clearer to me.

I am certain that there was more to this assignment than I may ever know, but what I do know is that I stepped into a divine moment and timing, and my obedience to do what God was leading me to do was vitally important. I don't know why He chose that specific place and that time, but He knows, and He graciously prodded me into that moment, and my life and ministry were forever changed.

We don't have to understand everything about God's leading, but we must obey Him whenever, however, and in whatever way He instructs because it matters when it's time. There is always purpose in His leading, and when He leads, we must use the sword of the Word of God to pierce through fear and hesitation, bringing every thought and emotion captive to the obedience of Christ so that we take those leaps of faith to obey Him. You may not know what's on the other side of your obedience, but you can rest assured that God does. The journey continues, and there are doors that are set before us that will lead to God's "next things." Faith pleases God. Our willingness to obey Him will be a key to unlock those doors of His intentions and to set necessary and timely things into motion for ourselves...and for others.

12

A Time of Launching

Trust God from the bottom of your heart; don't try to figure out everything on your own. Listen for God's voice in everything you do, everywhere you go; He's the One who will keep you on track.

—Proverbs 3:4-5

After years of working with teams on various projects in the nations and also ministering in church conferences and gatherings, my journey began to take yet another major turn in a direction that was completely unexpected. The Lord began to speak many prophetic words to me through several different trusted, seasoned people that He was going to begin to launch me into ministry in our nation, the United States of America. At that time, I had no way of knowing how this would ever come to pass, but the great Shepherd was guiding me, step by step.

At the end of 2016, the Lord instructed me to "connect" with a local church. That was His specific and exact word: "connect." So, the following Sunday, after hearing this instruction, I visited that church.

As I was on my way home from that meeting, I received a message from Apostle Randy Lopshire, via Facebook. He said, "I saw you at church this morning, but didn't get a chance to say hello. My wife, April, and I would love to 'connect' with you one day this week." While not an unusual word to use in this context, because of what the Lord had spoken to me earlier that week, I knew his use of the word "connect" was significant. It was God's way of saying to me, "You are on the right track." He was ordering my steps for His purposes.

Later that week, I did meet Randy and April for lunch. Our conversation provided the amazing discovery that our journeys and experiences with the Lord were shockingly similar. It was a true "God-connection!"

None of us realized how key this "connection" would be for our lives. God was working, and what He was doing was not just about us or about that particular moment. God was moving us down the path of His plan, and it was bigger than we could have even imagined. He was setting necessary things into motion that would launch us into His "now" identity for each of our lives and connect us to other people and other things that, at that time, were not even on our spiritual radars!

God Used a Dream

The three years that followed that initial "connection" with the Lopshire's were critical times along my journey. Each step was leading me toward a defining moment that would change everything.

One of the major ways the Lord speaks to me is through dreams and visions, and during that time, He began to give me more dreams that were specifically about the United States of America.

In February of 2018, I received a very important dream from the Lord concerning the verdict that He had determined for America. This dream, included in its entirety in my book, *Awakening the Church to Awaken a Nation*, revealed that the verdict had come as a result of prayer. The dream began in the setting of a national prayer gathering that was concluding. (This was an actual gathering that would be hosted by Dutch Sheets Ministries at the Trump Hotel in Washington, D.C. two weeks after I had this dream.)

In the dream, an angel emerged from that gathering with a scroll, which contained God's verdict. The angel took the scroll to the United States Capitol Building, entered the House Chambers, and before a very large crowd of people, including lawmakers, announced very loudly and emphatically, "The verdict has been determined: America shall be saved!"[1]

After having the dream, some of those close to me felt it would be good if I sent it to Dutch Sheets Ministries, since it involved the upcoming prayer gathering that they would be hosting in Washington, D.C. Apostle Dutch Sheets is an internationally known minister, author, and Bible teacher. He is also a well-respected apostolic voice and intercessory prayer leader in America. I was very reluctant and even a bit intimidated to send them the dream because, at that time, no one at Dutch's ministry knew me, nor had I ever met Dutch or his wife, Ceci, personally. I had only known of him by having read some books he had written and through some conferences where I had heard him speak. I imagined that he must receive thousands of emails, and to send him this dream would be meaningless. Then Holy Spirit arrested me one day as I was walking through my home. I distinctly heard this unction: "Send that dream to Dutch Sheets Ministries, and do it NOW!" It wasn't a suggestion; it was an urgent requirement. So, in obedience, I emailed a copy of the dream to DSM via their website. I never expected a reply, yet before the end of the day, I received one, thanking me for taking the time to send them the dream.

Two weeks later, I was literally about to step up to speak at a meeting, when I got a text from my mom. "Dutch Sheets is reading your dream at the Turn Around Conference in Washington, D.C. right now!" I could hardly believe what she was saying! That was amazing!

After the meeting, a friend of mine and I watched the replay of the conference. I was shocked that Dutch had read the dream, but more than that, I was deeply moved by the response of those in the congregation as he read it. There was thunderous applause and rejoicing from those devoted intercessors who had gathered for days in Washington, D.C. for the sole purpose of releasing a united appeal to Heaven on behalf of our nation. This dream revealed that God's response to that cry was His determined verdict to save America! In the dream, that verdict came at the very end of the prayer gathering, and in the literal gathering, the dream was the very last thing that Dutch shared.

For many months following, Dutch continued to read that dream all across America. My name had not been added as the dreamer of the dream–and that was fine by me. Dutch did not know who had sent it to them, but he knew it was a definite word from the Lord, and he continued to tell the dream. As he continued to share the dream, thousands of intercessors all across America devotedly came into agreement with God's will and verdict.

Another important thing that happened during this time, which may seem so small and insignificant, would prove to be a necessary step along the journey. During one of our conversations, I told Apostle Randy about Dutch Sheets, and I later gave him a book written by Apostle Tim Sheets, called, *Angel Armies*. That book deeply impacted

Randy, and the Lord eventually opened the way for him to meet Apostle Tim. That meeting opened an unexpected door that would change our lives forever.

Tim Sheets came to minister at our church in October of 2018, and God established a meaningful connection that was a part of a much bigger purpose than any of us could have even imagined. This was definitely an important step on the journey. We were not considering the future, we were just living in the moment, but all the while, God was looking ahead, and He was putting the pieces together. His plan wasn't just about us, a church, or a region. His plan was about the salvation of a nation, and He was launching us into position to take our place and to do our part in that part of His plan.

In August 2019, both Tim Sheets and Dutch Sheets were scheduled to speak at a weekend conference at our church. Two weeks prior to their coming, the Lord led me to gather intercessors from our region to pray for this conference. I felt deeply that the meetings would be timely and very strategic.

During the gathering of the intercessors, the Lord showed to me a quick vision. In the vision, I saw an American flag spread out, and there were two needles pulling thread into the flag. I heard the Lord say, "I am sewing you in to the fabric of what I am doing in this nation. It's time for your part. Others cannot be sewn in to do their part until I sew you in to do your part." I knew this was a powerful word for both our region/state and for myself. I was deeply impacted by the vision and by that word.

The following week at the conference, I was introduced to Dutch Sheets. Randy had told him that I was the one who had the "America Shall be Saved" dream. That introduction opened the way through which God began to connect me to many other people who would eventually help to launch me into a national ministry.

It's not that any of us as individuals are anything great or more important than others. Philippians 2:13 reveals that God works in us both to will and to do His good pleasure. God knows what is in us, and He knows how and when to join the parts to form the whole of His intentions. God was meticulously and purposefully joining us in the exact place to perform the exact function He wanted for that time (see 1 Corinthians 12:18). I have often said that where the plan of God is concerned, there are no big parts and no little parts; there are just parts. We each have a part, and every part matters.

He was "sewing us in to the fabric of what He was doing in this nation." He had said, "Others cannot be sewn in to do their part until I sew you in to do your part." What a profound revelation and realization of how intricately and meticulously God is working through each of us to fulfill His plans for our times! It is so important that we trust and allow Him to position us and work through us to do our part because there are others who can't get into their place until we get into our place. The parts make up the whole, and the whole never surfaces unless the parts are rightly put into place. Times of transition and positioning may not always be comfortable for our flesh, but when they come, they come because it's time. And at that moment in 2019, the Lord was announcing to me, "It's time for your part to be put into place."

That time of transition wasn't just happenstance, it was supernatural! It was the fulfillment of a prophetic revelation the Lord had given to me twelve years prior. I wrote the following in my book, *Awakening the Church to Awaken a Nation:*

> One of the most memorable moments in my life happened late one evening in a heavy rainstorm in June of 2007 as I was driving down the interstate outside of Nashville, Tennessee. The Lord visited me that night, right there in my car. At that moment, He spoke a profound word to me that stopped me in my tracks, literally! I pulled over to the side of the interstate, which is something I never do, and I sat in that car in the pouring down rain, with traffic speeding by, shaking my car, and for about thirty minutes, I wept uncontrollably in the power of His presence. He said to me, "I have raised you up to change a denomination." I knew He was speaking to me of the Church. The compassion I felt in His words that night and the certainty in which He spoke

awakened something deep inside me, and it changed me forever!

A few months later, He spoke this same word to me again, only this time He said, "I have raised you up to change a divided nation." I came to realize that God was revealing to me a two-fold mandate that I would have a part in: bringing change to the Church (denomination) and bringing change to the nation of the United States of America (a divided nation).

Let me just again interject here that I am in no way insinuating that I feel that I am greater than anyone else. None of us is an entity in and of ourselves. We are a body. However, there will come those moments when God begins to define to each of us our individual part, our place in the body, not for the purpose of exalting self, but rather for the building up of the body.

God was not saying to me that I was the only one who had been raised up for this purpose of changing the Church and the nation. He was saying that I had a place in that part of His plan.

There are no words to explain what I felt in both of those encounters. It was surreal and powerful as I was hearing God say to me, in essence, "I placed in you a purpose. I formed you with that purpose in mind. I have been moving you toward this moment, and now, I set you on the path to becoming what I've created you to be."

This was definitely a defining moment for me. This was not a pride thing. To be really honest, it wasn't even something that I fully welcomed at the time. I was completely undone, and my initial thoughts were more like those of Gideon's: *You must have the wrong person! Who am I that You should say such things to and about me? How could this be true?* My mind immediately began to try to figure out the "how" of this word. How could I change the Church or have an impact on a nation? What did that even mean? Nothing in my present moment seemed to indicate that this word could possibly be relevant for me, but many times, the word that the Lord gives is not always for the moment in which we hear it. Sometimes what He speaks is for an appointed time that is yet to come. God wasn't necessarily speaking about who I was; He was speaking about who I was becoming.

God is the Planner...and as we surrender ourselves to hear and follow Him, He will order our steps down the path of fulfilling the purpose and destiny He has designed for our lives. It is God's part to order our steps and plan our ways. It is our part to obediently step where He orders so that our lives can release the supply that He has placed in us that has to do with His plan in the time and place in which He has determined.

His word to me that rainy night in 2007 was not given for the purpose of saying, "Here's what I want. Now go do it," but God spoke those words in order to point me in a direction that I would never have been aware of, had He not spoken. The timing for the destiny was near, so God came to me ahead of time to awaken me to an awareness of the future that He had planned for my life. And though what I heard from the Lord that night wasn't anything at all like what I was seeing at the present time, His words gave me assurance and understanding that what I would experience in the days and years ahead would be the necessary process that would prepare me to be ready to step into the destiny when its time came.

God knows what we are capable of being and doing because He put that capability in us. He knows how to weave all the parts together to form the whole of His intended purposes. When destiny and timing meet, that's a defining moment, and when a defining moment occurs for us, God is not looking for our understanding; He's looking for our faith in Him and our willingness to obey Him.

As God's plan is unfolding, our place in that plan becomes necessary, and the timing of God begins to put pressure on those seeds of destiny that we carry. The only way to release the pressure is to surrender to God and to allow Him to reveal the purpose for which we were created. He awakens the seeds, not just hoping they can produce the desired fruit, but knowing they will produce because He is with us, empowering us to be all that He created us to be. And what God knows and can see is always so much more than we can think or imagine.

When God began unfolding the unforeseen future that He had planned for my life, I never thought that the sharing of the dreams, visions, and prophetic words, that come to me from the Lord through divine influence would be one of the avenues through which He would reveal and release His purposes. But God knows the plans He has for us, and He knows exactly how to work those plans to bring forth His destiny in each of our lives....

I had spent many years teaching and preaching the Word of God. Along the way, the prophetic ministry began to increase and develop in my life. Dreams and visions began to come to me more often and in greater detail. Prophetic words would flow through me as I preached, taught, and

> prayed. Though I didn't even realize it at the time, the process of "becoming" was happening. God was ordering my steps. I saw where I was; He saw where I was going. He was putting together all of the pieces, connecting me to the right people, and giving me the necessary experiences that were building wisdom, character, and understanding that would be beneficial for the destiny He was moving me toward.[2]

And what an amazing journey it has been! God saw what was ahead. He had orchestrated every component and strategically guided me every step of the way. Obedience to visit a church led to the gifting of a book that led to a meeting that led to a dream that led to a connection that led to a timely positioning for God's purposes—steps on the journey—and every step mattered.

The journey has been happening for all of us, and now we are finding ourselves in a new era, in which He is revealing the purpose for many of our steps. Those steps are "stitches" in time that God has been using to "sew us in" to the destiny for which that journey has been preparing us.

Just before that major transitional moment in 2019 when God began to launch me into a national ministry, the Spirit of the Lord spoke to me and said:

> Your life is about to change. There are connections being made even now that will be instrumental in shifting you into your "appointed

place." What has seemed an unattainable dream will now open before you. You must stay dependent on Me, or else what comes will close as fast as it opens! This is not the time to lean on your own understanding because this is far above your ability to imagine. I Am doing this! I see it all, and I know how to order your steps. Don't assume that you know; you don't. But I will order your steps, and teach you how to walk in this place I have assigned for you. You've never passed this way before. You have seen it in part by My Spirit, but it is far greater than you know. It is connected to many other things that I Am and have been doing. I Am putting the pieces together!

Your trust and dependence on Me will lead you to obedience, and your obedience is the key that will get you through this door. Decisions must be made, not rationalized through your carnal reasoning. Listen to Me! Move when I say move! Do what I tell you to do! Don't judge things with your natural reasoning. Look in the Spirit! I Am working this out! It's My plan, and I tell you, the parts are being connected. This is what you have been waiting for, but don't misjudge it by filtering it through your understanding. You thought you knew, but My thoughts are so much higher than your thoughts. You only see in part. I see the whole! You fit! You have a place! Don't walk by assumption! Listen to Me intentionally...I Am

> about to position you. Things are coming together!

The Lord knows every step we are to take on our journey. He knows the "how," and He knows the "when." He has promised to order our steps. Do not lose heart along the journey. Things are happening that are important pieces to a much larger picture. A dear friend often says to me, "God is doing more than one thing at a time." If we do not grow weary and faint or give up along the journey, we will enter those moments when all of the pieces will come together, and we will see with greater clarity why each step was necessary.

Another key word the Lord spoke to me during that time is something I feel is very fitting to include in this chapter. Hear Him! Be encouraged and know that the great Shepherd has charted your course. His plan is unfolding, and He will rightly position you in order to see that plan fulfilled. Trust Him and follow His lead.

> There is a path coming into view. It is the "way" that I (the Lord) have chosen for you. Your steps are being ordered supernaturally. There is a yielding on your part that will be required—a surrender to Me! But as you step where I order, you will find a courage that will rise in you that you have never known before. It is courage that will flow out of the wisdom and understanding that will be released as you venture down this path.

I Am touching your eyes. I Am giving you eyes to see. You will understand and see and know! And courage will flow, and you will go in My strength with My wisdom and My vision, and you will be empowered to accomplish what you've never accomplished before! You will be what you've been becoming! You are being cloaked with your new identity. Receive it by faith, and what you receive by faith now will manifest in the days to come.

Things will become clearer and clearer to you as you move forward with Me! Opportunities, connections, provisions, vision—it's all on the path! As you yield to Me and allow Me to define you and to direct your steps, your thoughts, your actions, then I will reach through you and make Myself known! The path is forming before you. I am giving you eyes to see it and to step into it by faith. My manifested presence is on that path. To walk it is to walk with Me. You will see it by the Spirit, and as it is revealed, be bold and courageous and take the first steps. Don't look back. Stay focused on Me! This is the opening of your new day.

I feel that the Body of Christ is being called to another level of engagement, requiring sensitivity to the Holy Spirit and remaining in a consistent readiness to advance. We must know and be completely persuaded that the Spirit of the Lord is upon us, anointing us for this moment!

The Lord has need of us. I heard the Spirit of the Lord say that there are going to be moments in the days ahead when He's going to speak to us, and He's going to give us information, assignments, and prayer directives. He's going to lead us and order our steps for His purposes, but if we're not alert, we'll just keep doing what we've been doing, praying what we've been praying, staying caught up in the routine motion. But something's changing, and we need to receive what God is pouring out as He anoints us and sends us out as a prepared people ready to move into a prepared moment.

God has purpose for all of us, and it's not like a one-time thing. Purpose is whatever God wants done in a specific moment. If we are the ones that He chooses to work through, then He will put it in our spirit to do it. Whatever it is—a prayer He wants prayed, a person He wants you to call on the phone, a decree He wants you to make, a place He wants you to go—whatever it is in that moment, there is purpose in it, and we must be sensitive to Holy Spirit so that we hear the Lord correctly and respond to Him swiftly with obedience.

We are the conduits through which He speaks and works. He has called us on purpose for His purposes. Obedience is key. In this moment the Lord is requiring things of us. He is awakening things in us, connecting us to the right people, and He is revealing necessary things to us. We must watch Him, hear and obey Him, and follow His leading so that His intentions and purposes can be fulfilled in their right timing.

13

Provision

But my God shall supply all your need according to His riches in glory by Christ Jesus.

—Philippians 4:19 KJV

I was taught from an early age that where God guides, you can always trust Him to provide. I have definitely experienced the reality of this statement throughout my life!

I have many stories that I could tell of how I have personally experienced God's supernatural provision, but for now, I will only share a few.

I will start with one story that not only taught me about receiving but also was an unforgettable lesson that demonstrated the importance of giving, as described in Luke 6:38: "Give and it will be given to you..."

In my very early twenties, I was introduced to a powerful woman of God, who travelled the world to preach and teach the Gospel. This lady was very instrumental in my life at that time, and I learned so much from observing her strong faith and the impacts of that faith on her own life. Her knowledge of the Word of God challenged me to dig into the deeper things of God's Word and discover its truths for myself.

Through her teaching and living example, the Lord opened my understanding of things I had never known before. One of those things was the principle of sowing and reaping. I know that's a controversial subject to some, but let me preface this by saying, that I am not a "name it, claim it" type of believer. My understanding of this concept is not so much about a "give to get" motive, but more that my obedience in giving is part of my worship to the Lord. Just as He leads us in assignments and other ways, He also leads us concerning how to be good stewards of our money, possessions, and even our time. This is a much larger subject than I want to cover in this book, but I do challenge you to open your heart to hear God concerning stewardship of these things. It does matter to Him, and there are undeniable blessings that are attached to our obedience in giving.

One Sunday afternoon, this particular minister announced that she was planning to go on an overseas ministry trip. As she spoke of her agenda for that trip, the Lord strongly dealt with me about sowing financial seed into that project. I felt He was leading me to give fifty dollars a week for the four weeks leading up to her trip. I was overjoyed to know that I would have the opportunity to be a part of such a wonderful ministry endeavor.

However, I only had a part-time job at the time, which paid very little. I cleaned the home of a lady who owned a preschool in our rural county. I worked one day a week, and my pay was not enough to fulfill the commitment the Lord was asking me to make. I had no idea where I would come up with the money, but I was certain that I had heard Him correctly. So, I prayed something along these lines, "Lord, You know that I will give You whatever You ask, but what You have asked is more than what I have, so I need You to provide so that I can give."

As that week progressed, leading up to the next Sunday when I would begin to give my first fifty-dollar offering, I continued to pray for God's intervention. With my paycheck that week, I would have the first offering, but for the weeks that would follow, I knew I wouldn't have enough.

After cleaning the lady's house that next Friday morning, I went into her office to receive my check from her. When she gave me the check, she asked if I had a moment to talk with her. I don't know why, but my first thought was that she was going to say she didn't need me to clean for her anymore, and my heart sank a little. Instead, she told me that she had been thinking about creating a teaching position for me in her preschool, and she wanted to know how I felt about that. She said, "The pay won't be much at first, but if things work out, I might be able to increase it later on. I will still need and will pay you the same for the cleaning job, but for the next few weeks, I will also start you out as a part-time teacher, on a trial basis, and for that, I will pay you an additional fifty dollars each week."

I don't know if she could see it in my eyes, but my spirit was rejoicing with great joy! Jehovah Jireh had created a position just for me, and the pay was the exact amount that I needed for the weekly offering He had asked me to give. I was beyond excited to get to church the next few weeks!

Little did I know that trial basis would lead to a full-time teaching position that would become a training ground to prepare me for future assignments that the Lord would lead me to do! The joy of partnering with the Lord through my giving was so exciting for me. Knowing Him as Jehovah Jireh has built a deep faith in me that has benefited me throughout my life!

What about the Money?

I have encountered the Lord as Provider many times in my life. One major encounter that comes to mind is when I knew for certain that I would be going to Central America to serve as a young missionary, teaching in a school. I began the process of preparation for that upcoming assignment. I met with all the necessary people to get approved as a teacher for the organization I would be working through, made arrangements for my travel, gathered all the supplies that I could think of that would be necessary for my time there, and packed my bags for the trip.

The day before I was to leave, I was in my living room checking and rechecking all of my luggage, when I received a telephone call from the General Director of the mission organization. He was encouraging me on my upcoming adventure, and he prayed for me. Then, just before he ended the call, he said, "O, by the way, you will need to send us a check for four hundred dollars. Just drop it in the mail before you leave tomorrow. This will cover your first month's rent and board." With that, the call ended, and fear and doubt rushed over me like a strong ocean wave.

I looked at my mom and told her what he said. Then out of my mouth flowed these words, "Where in the world am I going to get $400...before morning?" It wasn't so much a question as it was a statement of doubt. I had been so excited. I was one day away, and now it seemed that with one phone call, all of my hopes and expectations had been dashed. Just like that, everything seemed to come to a screeching halt.

I went to my bedroom, threw myself across the bed and wept. "God, I don't understand. Why had I not been informed of this earlier? Now it's too late. I have no way to get four hundred dollars before morning. I just don't understand!"

After a few moments, I sat up on the side of the bed, looked over to my nightstand, and saw a Bible. It was The Living Bible translation, and without even knowing why, I reached over and picked it up. That Bible literally fell open to Second Chronicles, chapter twenty-five. It wasn't an intentional "flop-and-drop" on my part—like when some people let the Bible flop open and drop their finger on a verse without looking, hoping to read something that will minister to them—but I'm certain that it was intentional on God's part! I looked down at the page, and it seemed all the words were blurred, except for one portion of the chapter, and these words seemed to be highlighted: "'But the money!' Amaziah whined. 'What shall I do about that?' And the prophet replied, 'The Lord is able to give you much more than this'" (2 Chronicles 25:9 TLB)!

Those words shot through me like an arrow, and instantly, I heard the Lord say to me, "Gina, if you can't believe Me for $400, then you have no business going to the mission field. Trust Me! I Am able to give you that and so much more!"

I stood up, wiped my eyes, marched myself back into the living room and finished packing my suitcases. A couple of hours later, I got ready and went to church. It would be a long time before I would be able to attend my home church again, so it was a special night for me.

I had no idea, but the congregation had planned a going-away party for me after the meeting that night. They had a cake made for me and gave me some gifts. There were lots of hugs and tears, and some of what people respectfully refer to as "holy handshakes." (You would experience one such handshake when someone wants to give you a monetary gift without making a big deal out of it. They shake your hand to slip the money from their hand to yours.) After each of the handshakes, I hugged and thanked them, and without looking at the amount, I just put the money into my pocket. When I got home that night, I counted the money, and the total amount was six hundred dollars! It was more than what I even needed!

God is so faithful! Even when we whine, He still provides!

Look Again

I quickly found that living on the mission field requires more than just a calling and a heart to serve; it takes money, too. Rent, food, supplies...all of these things are the missionary's personal responsibility. I started my time as a missionary with two hundred dollars and the spiritual lesson the Lord had taught me the night before I left home. I had been armed with an unshakeable revelation of God's provision, and that revelation proved to be invaluable during my time on the mission field.

About three months after I arrived, I was faced with a situation that required me to put that lesson into action. I had just finished teaching my morning classes, and I had gone back to my house and was sitting on the front porch. I was enjoying some ice-cold watermelon in an attempt to cool off from the extreme heat and humidity, when I received a visit from our office manager. She came to inform me that my rent and gas payments were due. If I were not able to pay them, I would more than likely have to leave my position because the school just didn't have the funds to support me financially.

That morning I had just checked my bank account back home, and I knew there was no money for the payment. I told her that I did not have the money, and I asked if she could give me until the end of the day to let her know what I would do. "Of course," she said, "Check your account again. You never know, something may come in."

After she left, I went and knelt beside my bed and prayed about the situation. I then went back to teach my afternoon classes. After the last class, I stopped by the office to check my bank account again, but still, no funds were available. On the walk back to my house, I just calmly said to the Lord, "You called me here, and I know it. You said it would be for a short while, so if this is the end of my time here, then that's okay, but if I'm not done, then I ask that You make a way for me to stay."

That evening, the office manager came by my house to bring some copies of test papers that I had asked her to print for me. We chatted a moment, and then she said, "O, by the way, your rent and gas payments have been paid."

I could hardly believe what I heard, and I said, "How is that possible? I just checked my account, and there was nothing in there!"

She said, "I received a call from the home office this afternoon to let me know that a family in the States had been led by the Lord to sell a family heirloom. They divided the money they received from the sale into several parts to be given to different missionaries. This couple saw your name on a list of missionaries, and they felt that you were one who should receive part of the money. It was enough to cover your rent and then some. I used some to pay your rent and gas payments, and the rest is in your account. So, look again, and you'll find the account is not empty!"

I ran to the office to check my account and found the surplus! Only God could work such a timely miracle! He saw and supplied my need. I called, and He answered. I never knew who that couple was, and they did not know me. God drew their attention to my name, and they gave. I am certain that God blessed them for their obedience and that their seed was multiplied back to them! That's just how He works! He is faithful always and in all ways!

Before You Call

Another experience I had during my time in Central America left a deep impression on me that I have never forgotten. I was again needing money for my rent and gas payments, but the funds just were not available. I knew the payments were coming due. I also knew there was nothing that I could do within my own ability, so I prayed about it, went about my duties, and left the matter in God's hands. I did not tell anyone about the needed funds.

We didn't have cell phones at that time. We had a landline, and long-distance calls to home could quickly add up to a small fortune! We also had email, but those could also be a bit costly, as they had to be sent via dial-up connection—a very slow dial-up connection—which was also a constant test of my patience. Therefore, communications with those back home were not as frequent as I would have preferred. When the telephone did ring, it could be a bit startling!

One night, late in the evening, my telephone rang, and I answered to find it was my mom calling. It was so great to hear her voice and to catch up with what was going on at home, but this call wasn't just for the purpose of casual conversation. She had called to tell me that a friend of mine felt that the Lord had led her to have a benefit singing for me at our church, and they had done so that night. The singing had just ended. Momma said, "It snowed, so not a lot of people were able to come, but they collected some money for you, and I wanted you to know that I will be putting it in your account tomorrow." When she told me the amount they had raised, I cried! It was the EXACT amount that I needed...to the penny!

I learned that the singing had been planned for several weeks. Even before I had called, the Lord was already at work to provide.

God Never Ceases to Amaze Me

About a year after I returned home from my time in Central America, I felt the Lord was leading me to another location. This time it was to the state of Montana. I had never been out west, and honestly, at that time, I really didn't know much about Montana. So, I got a map and began to familiarize myself with the names of some of the cities there. Again, there were no cell phones at that time, so no map apps were available. The map I used was a large paper atlas. As I looked at that map, I asked the Lord where He wanted me to go. I didn't know anyone there, but I was certain this was the leading of the Lord, and I knew He would make clear to me the path forward.

I felt impressed to call the headquarters of the denomination that I was affiliated with at that time. The lady I talked with was so excited to hear my story of how the Lord was calling me to go to Montana. She said that the only thing she knew to do was to connect me with the presiding overseer of the state, and maybe he could help me. So, I called the overseer, and he first asked me if I wanted to pastor a church there. They were in desperate need of pastors. I really didn't know what God was sending me there to do, but I did not feel a call to pastor, and I told him so. All I knew was that I was supposed to go. So, he gave me the number of a local pastor in Billings and told me to call him. I called the pastor and told him my story. He said, "You may not believe this, but I was just sitting here praying and asking the Lord to send us helpers to this city." He was overcome with encouragement and thanked me for my obedience.

That pastor became my only contact in Montana. We set up a time and date when I could come and meet with him and his wife. Getting there would be no small feat. It took us several weeks to prepare. I met with my family to tell them what God was calling me to do. After much discussion, they all decided they were to go with me on this first visit. So, I rented a vehicle, which was a first for me at the time, and with my large paper atlas, I mapped out the journey. It would take us two days, driving long hours to get there. Gas, food, hotels...and you guessed it, I didn't have the money, but I had an assurance that "Where God guides, He provides." This was now a tried and proven reality for me.

There are too many details to share about how the money came, but just in time, God saw to it that we had more than enough to make the trip.

I have never experienced such cold temperatures as we experienced on that trip. It was dangerously cold that year, with actual temperatures dipping way below zero. It was difficult to be outside the car for more than a few minutes. Crazy cold! My nephew, who was seven years old at the time, was with us on this trip. We had not anticipated such cold weather, and for some reason, we had forgotten to bring him a pair of gloves. Stopping at a travel center to get gas, my mom had mentioned that we needed to find and purchase some gloves for him. As she was saying this to my dad, she looked out her window, and right beside her door she saw a glove lying in the snow!

She opened the door and got it. Then something lying on the ground at a phone booth next to us caught my eye. I went to see what it was, and to my amazement, it was the matching glove! The gloves looked brand new, and they fit my nephew perfectly! It was as if they had been placed there just for him, and I believe they were. God sees and knows all things, and He is a wonderful provider!

I will be honest and tell you there were moments when I had some serious talks with the Lord and with myself as we drove those many miles. Those talks always included this question, "What are we doing?!" In the natural, it seemed foolish. It looked foolish, and it felt foolish! But in the spirit, we heard His call, "Come, follow Me," and that call was a force greater than the cold or any other obstacle that may have presented itself. We were determined to make it to our destination.

When we finally arrived at our location, all I had was an address where we would meet with the pastor and his wife. We still had no GPS–only the paper map–and we did our best to navigate, but we got lost. We kept circling the same block, over and over. It was so bizarre that no matter what street we took, we kept coming back to that same block.

Finally, we somehow made it out of that downtown location and found our way to the church. In the parking lot, there was a vehicle with a U-Haul trailer attached to it. I went inside to find the pastor that I had spoken with on the telephone. To my shock, he had forgotten all about our call, and was, at first, puzzled as to who I was and why I was there. He finally remembered our conversation but told me that he and his wife had decided to accept a church in another state, and that morning was their last day in Montana.

This was my only contact, so I had no idea where to go or what to do. At the end of our conversation, the pastor told me of a street ministry that was located downtown. He was sure that they would need some help, so he called the director of the ministry and told him we would be stopping by. He gave me the address and sent us on our way. We had no problem finding the address, for it was the exact block that we had circled so many times when we first arrived! We had gotten "lost" at the location where we would be serving in the months ahead. God never ceases to amaze me.

We met the directors of the mission and my brother, sister-in-law, nephew, and I wound up going back there to serve for about five months. This was another piece of the puzzle that God was putting together for my life. I learned a lot during my time there, and though it was short, it was an important step on my journey.

Every Need Supplied

In June of that same year, while still living in Montana, I received a call from a minister friend of mine who lived in Tennessee. He felt the Lord was leading him to take a team of people for an evangelism trip to Belize. Since I had lived there for a short while, he asked if I would be willing to go with them to help lead the trip. If not, he asked if I could at least come and meet with the team. I told him that I didn't have the money to make the mission trip, but I would be willing to come and meet with him and the team. So, we packed everything up to make the trip back home.

Several weeks prior to this trip, I had dreamed that I was in a location standing next to someone on a platform. Suddenly, in the dream, hundreds of people lined up in front of me. I asked the person next to me in the dream who all these people were. He said, "They are here for you. They've come to bless you."

The man then led me off the platform, and one by one, those people began to come to me and place money in my hands. And that was the end of the dream.

I later told my sister-in-law about this dream, and we both giggled and said, "Wouldn't that be something!"

We made the trip back to Tennessee to meet with the team that was going to Central America for the mission project. My friend, who would be leading the mission team, was, at that time, preaching in a revival about two and a half hours from my mom's house where I was staying. So, my mom, my sister-in-law, a friend, and I drove to that location. We arrived early so that I could meet with the team. The meeting went well, and then we decided to stay for that night's revival service.

During the service, the minister went to the microphone and called me to come to the front for prayer. I walked up to the front, facing him, and he began to tell the congregation that I was a missionary. He also told them of the upcoming mission project he was leading and that I had served as a teacher at the location where they were going, so he really wanted me to go with them but I didn't have the funds to make the trip. He wanted everyone to stretch their hands toward me and pray that if God wanted me to go, He would provide the money for me.

As he and the congregation prayed, I felt such a weighty presence of the Lord come over me! It's hard to articulate, but I felt as if I were being surrounded by the presence of God, and I began to sob. I am not one who cries a lot, but when I feel His precious presence, it always moves me to tears! I stood there engulfed in this powerful encounter, and the next thing I knew, I felt someone putting what I thought was tissues in my hand.

I then heard my sister-in-law's voice over the sound system saying, "She had a dream about this!" I opened my eyes, and there were lines of people, coming one by one, and placing money in my hands. Someone brought some buckets and told me to drop the money in them. I hadn't even realized it, but my hands were filled with cash. I asked my friend what was happening, and he said, "While I was praying, the people just came forward to bless you and give so that you could join our team for this project [in Belize]."

Later that night, when the money was fully counted, it came to the exact amount that was needed...again, to the penny!

When we left the meeting that night, we were all so excited and amazed by what the Lord had just done. It was very late, and we still had the two-and-a-half-hour drive back to my mom's, but just after we started, the Lord began to speak to me. The others in the car were still talking about the exciting things we had just witnessed at the revival meeting, but it was as if I were caught up in the Spirit...and I was driving! I suddenly knew that I was to give part of that money to a lady who was leaving the next morning to go on a mission trip to Africa.

She lived near my mom, so we were still a few hours from her house. Since there were no cell phones at that time, I searched to find a pay phone so I could call her to let her know that I needed to come by her house before she left for the trip. I found a pay phone and pulled up beside it, but there was one problem: I did not know her phone number! I had never called her home before. So, I prayed, and as I prayed, a phone number came into my mind. I inserted my quarter into the slot on the pay phone, and I dialed the number. To my amazement, the woman's daughter answered! Isn't it amazing that God is so involved in our lives that He knows even the most minute details about us!

I told the daughter what was happening, and she gave the phone to her mom. I began to tell her what the Lord was leading me to do, when suddenly the phone went silent, and then there was a dial tone. I had not written the phone number down, and they had no way of reconnecting with me. What should I do? I suddenly remembered the number and redialed it. The daughter answered again. She apologized for the hang-up and explained that her mother was so overcome with thanksgiving to the Lord that she fell on her knees to praise Him, and without realizing what she was doing, she had hung up the phone!

The daughter then continued to tell me that she and her mom had been having a snack before they were to leave and drive to the airport in a few hours. As they were sitting there, the daughter had asked her mom how much money she had to take with her on the trip. Her mother didn't respond, and the daughter said, "You don't have any money, do you?" Her mom said, "God will provide." The lady's daughter then told me that as soon as those words left her mother's mouth, the telephone rang. She then said, "It was you on the other end, telling us that God had led you to give her some money for her trip."

For the next three hours, I drove as fast as I could, and we arrived at the lady's home just as they were putting her luggage in the car to leave for the airport. The Spirit of the Lord told me the amount to give to her. I gave it, and she was on her way. God had provided for her, just in time!

Later that night, I realized that giving the money to the lady now meant that I wouldn't have enough to pay for my trip to Central America with the team, and that's what the offering had been given for! But there was peace in my heart, and I was certain that God must have a plan!

The next day was Sunday, so I decided to attend a church in the area. No one at that church knew that I was home or that I would be visiting there, but during the meeting, the pastor's wife went to the front and said, "This morning before I came to church, the Lord spoke to me and said that we were to take up an offering for Gina, so let's do that now."

Once again God proved His faithfulness as my Provider! When the offering was counted, it was the exact amount that I had given to the missionary for her trip, which was the exact amount to replenish what I needed for my trip. He never ceases to amaze me!

I purchased my airline ticket and joined the team to Central America for a two-week evangelism project that was filled with miraculous happenings and was one of the most powerful times I had ever experienced up to that point on my journey.

The miracle didn't end there. Being on that team also connected me with people who would become lifelong friends and very important parts of my journey. Those connections were actually used by God to position me for the future that was continuing to unfold, and I can honestly say that I would not be where I am today, nor would I be doing what I am doing today, if it had not been for that trip and for those connections! As Ms. Billye Brim often says, "O, what a plan. O, what a Planner!"

When We Call, He Answers

It always amazes me how deeply the Lord cares for us and how involved and invested He is in our lives. He watches over us, and He loves us. O, how He loves us! He is our Father, and He invites us to come boldly to His throne of grace to obtain mercy and find grace to help in our times of need (see Hebrews 4:16). There is no need too small or too great. We can cast our cares onto Him, and He knows how and is willing to take care of us. He is our Provider.

Several years ago, I was in desperate need of a dependable vehicle. The car I had at the time, let's just say, ran more on prayer and faith than it did on gasoline. It wasn't a great car, and it certainly wasn't pretty to look at, but it got me where I had needed to go. However, its retirement years had come, no doubt about it.

Even back then, I was traveling a lot for ministry purposes, so when I would be called to go long distances, I would always have to rent a car to get me there. The Bible teaches us that we are to be "anxious for nothing, but in everything, by prayer and supplication, with thanksgiving, let [our] requests be made known to God" (Philippians 4:6 NKJV). Paul had obviously never ridden down the road in my car! If he had, he might have slightly reworded this verse a bit. It may have read more like, "Be anxious for nothing, unless you are riding in an unpredictable vehicle, then be concerned a bit, but not in fear," or something to that effect.

In all seriousness, I knew that God knew that I needed a newer vehicle. I didn't make a public announcement that I needed a car, nor had I asked for money to purchase one. I prayed about it, and as Paul instructed, I allowed the peace of God, which passes understanding to keep my heart and mind through Christ Jesus (see Philippians 4:7).

One Sunday afternoon, I had returned home from church and had just finished eating lunch with some friends when the telephone rang. When I answered the phone, I could hear someone on the other end of the line mumbling some words I could not understand. She was crying, and my first thought was that something was horribly wrong. But soon she regained her composure and said, "Sister Gina, I sat down to eat my lunch, and the Lord began to speak to me as I was praying over my food. His presence was so strong, and He talked to me about you. I could not eat anything until I called you to tell you what He said. He told me that I was to buy a car for you!" Well, now, we both were crying! She told me the amount of money that the Lord had put in her heart to give to me so that I could purchase a used car. The amount had been given to her through an inheritance that she had recently received, and God told her to give it all to me. I didn't know what to say. I was so humbled by such a selfless act of giving, and so deeply appreciative to God and to this precious lady through whom He was working to supply my need.

He knows everything about us. He sees our every need, and when we call to Him, He will answer us. And this miracle wasn't just about meeting my need, He was also working on behalf of the lady who gave. "Give, and it will be given to you. A good measure, pressed down, shaken together, running over will be poured into your lap. For with the measure you use, it will be measured to you" (Luke 6:38 NIV). Brother R.W. Shambach used to say, "You cannot outgive God." God worked to supply my need, and with the same measure of kindness, I am certain that He also worked on behalf of the lady who gave in order to restore and multiply back to her above and beyond what she had given. He's a good, good Father!

"I Stand in Awe of You"

On another occasion, years after that experience, God surprised me again with another incredible gift!

I received a call from a friend of mine who lives in another state. She and her husband wanted to know if I would be willing to meet them at a location in Ohio on a Saturday evening. We would spend the night there and then attend the Sunday morning service at an amazing church that was in the area. I agreed to the meeting.

We met for supper that Saturday evening. I had not seen them in a while, so it was so good to visit with them. After we ate, we remained at the table just catching up and talking about some of the adventures we've had together in ministry.

Then, out of the blue, my friend looked at me and said, "We want to tell you why we are really here." I was very puzzled and had no idea what was going on. At that point, she slid an envelope across the table and said, "This is why we wanted to meet with you." I opened the envelope, and it said something about a DMV registration or something. Seeing the confusion on my face, her husband said, "Here!" and he threw me a set of car keys. "God told us to give you our car!" I almost fell out of my chair! I was so humbled and so overcome with gratitude for this precious gift!

The restaurant was packed, but I didn't care! I jumped out of my seat and ran and hugged them both. I'm certain some may have thought I was crazy, but that didn't matter to me. I threw my hands in the air and thanked God, and over and over I thanked my friends for their amazing obedience to God and for their generosity!

I went back to my hotel room that night, and with my hands raised to God, from the depths of my heart, I sang to Him over and over this line from a song written in 1986 by Mark Altrogge: "I stand, I stand in awe of You!"

Growth Through Obedience

Through every experience I have had with the Lord, I have grown in my relationship with Him by leaps and bounds. The old folks used to say that experience is the best teacher, and it is so true. There are things that we will only learn about God as we experience Him for ourselves. Learning to trust Him with my money, my time, and my life has enabled me to receive countless blessings of divine favor, protection, prosperity, and to have a deeper relationship with Jesus! I have grown in wisdom and understanding, and also in my ability to hear His voice more clearly.

Deuteronomy 28:1-10 reveals the many benefits and blessings that will come on us and overtake us when we obey God's voice. He is a good Father, and He wants us to experience His goodness. He wants us to know Him by experience. As we obey Him, our lives are more deeply impacted by His abundance.

If I had not trusted Him to provide for me, I would still be living in lack. If I had not trusted Him to protect me, I would still be living in bondage to fear. If I hadn't taken those leaps of faith, I would never have known the joys and blessings that have come on me and overtaken me along my journey. And I'm still traveling, and I'm still experiencing Him in His goodness, favor, and power!

God's unlimited supply is on the path that He has chosen for us, and as we walk that path in obedience to Him, He will see to it that we lack nothing. Jesus still can make ways out of no way, and God is still Jehovah Jireh, our Provider!

14

Protection

The Lord will protect you from all evil; He will keep your life. The Lord will guard your going out and your coming in [everything that you do] from this time forth and forever.

—Psalm 121:7-8 AMP

Many of us can testify of the intervention of God as He spared us from hurt, harm, or injury. His eye is upon us, ever watching over us to keep and guard us, even sometimes when we are completely unaware of any danger at all. Yahweh is our great defender.

In this chapter, I will share with you a few experiences that I have had as a result of God's supernatural protection.

A Narrow Miss

One of those experiences happened as I was driving down the highway with my mom and dad several years ago. We were on our way to a prayer meeting. Just ahead, we were approaching an intersection. In the turn lane to my left was a man driving a huge dump truck with his turn signal on, waiting to cross the road in front of us. There was a man driving a car that was coming from the road on my right, and just as I approached the intersection, the man in the car pulled right out into my lane. Although I wasn't speeding, still I was going too fast to get stopped in time, and with a large truck in the turn lane to my left, there was absolutely nowhere for me to go. I remember I cried out, "Jesus!"

The next thing I knew, we were on the other side of the intersection. The large dump truck was still in the turn lane, and the man in the car was now behind me! I have no idea how He did it, but the Lord somehow pressed us between that dump truck and car without our hitting or even touching either vehicle or He helped us to pass through them. All I know is, it was supernatural. Jesus came to our defense as a shield, and He protected us from harm, and possibly even death.

Miracle on the Bridge

Another experience that I had in which the Lord protected me was during a time while on a mission trip. Arriving in a foreign country is often a rigorous venture passing through security lines getting your passport stamped, retrieving your checked luggage, going through customs, making your way through the crowds to find your awaiting hosts, and finally loading all of the luggage onto vans or trucks and making your way to your final destination.

On one particular trip, our team and I had gone through all of those steps, then hopped on the van for the hour-long drive to the base location where we would be staying for the next several days. Our lodging quarters were located in a remote village that was only accessible, at that time, by ferry boat or a primitive swinging, walk bridge. It was late in the evening and already getting dark, so the ferry was shut down for the night. That meant we would have to carry all of our luggage by hand across the swinging bridge that was high above a wide river.

The bridge was comprised of four steel cables—two for our hands to hold onto, and two beneath our feet that supported narrow slats of wood for us to step on. Each slat of wood was spaced about eight or ten inches apart. Those pieces of wood were the only things separating us from the drop to the river below!

Having a large team and a lot of luggage to transport across the bridge, we were making many trips, back and forth. Again, it was late in the evening, and it was starting to get dark. The only light we had was a street light that was situated at only one end of the bridge.

Just as we made the last trip across the bridge and were loading our luggage onto the next van, a young man came running toward me with something in his hand. "Miss Gina! Miss Gina! Your passport! You dropped your passport on the bridge!"

At the airport, I had thought I placed my passport safely back into my belly bag, but apparently, instead of placing it into the zipper pocket, I had unknowingly placed it between the bag and my belt. As we were making our way across the bridge, the passport had fallen out from that unsecured place. How I had not lost it prior to boarding the van at the airport, and how the young man saw it in the dark, I will never know. And, perhaps, the greatest miracle was that with as much foot traffic as was taking place that evening, the passport had remained on the bridge on one of those narrow slats without falling into the river. That was definitely a wonder!

Not having a passport in a foreign country, especially during that time, could have led to a very serious situation, but God was watching over me to guard and protect me.

Momma's Prayers

Another encounter that I had with the protection of the Lord happened while I was living as a missionary in another country. I lived alone in a house on the campus of a school that was located in a remote area. It was a beautiful setting on the banks of a river and surrounded by lush, thick jungle. The dirt road that made its way through the school's property continued on for about a mile or so, leading to a church and then to the campus of a YWAM discipleship training school.

A young missionary, who was temporarily staying at the school, and I had decided to start getting up early in the morning and walking down that road to the church and back. It was so refreshing to walk along and enjoy the peaceful calm and cool morning air before the day would succumb to the noise of students and the near unbearable daytime heat. We took this walk for several mornings.

One morning, before the sun rose, I was awakened by the sound of the school's director banging his hand on the wall outside my house. He said very sternly, "Gina, get up, get dressed, and get down to our house!" A sudden wave of fear swept over me. I knew something was seriously wrong.

I did as he instructed, and when I arrived at their home, I found our director and three other lady missionaries gathered in the living room. Our director informed us that about an hour prior to that moment, a lady who was a part of a team that was working out of the church just down the road from our school had been kidnapped and raped. The rapist was on the run, and the authorities believed that he was in the jungle near our school. Our director's wife was a nurse, and she had been called to go to the hospital to help the rape victim. The director felt it was best for the other staff members and me to gather at their home for protection.

Later that evening, the rapist was located. The police encircled his camp and took him into custody. He confessed to the crime, giving details of all that happened.

We were told that the threat of harm had passed, and it was safe for us to return to our homes. We were all relieved that the threat of harm was over, and I was glad to be back safely in my home, but sleep was not to be had. It was very late into the night, and I was sitting on the side of my bed, reflecting on the happenings of the day. Suddenly, I was startled by the ringing of the telephone. We only had a landline phone at that time, and a late-night call was very rare. I answered the call and experienced a wave of comfort when I heard my momma's voice on the other end of the line. She said that she had tried all that day to call, but the lines were not working and she couldn't get through. She had called to check on me because late the night before, she had had a bad dream in which she had somehow gotten information that someone was planning to rape me! When she awakened from that dream she immediately began to pray for my protection. For the rest of the night and throughout that day, she and my daddy had continued to pray. They prayed until they felt a release in the spirit.

They had known absolutely nothing about what had happened that day, but God knew, and He had alerted them ahead of time to pray for my protection. We would later learn just how accurate that dream had been and how important those prayers were.

The following morning, a young man, who at one time had been a student at our school, came by to inform us that he had been the one to lead the police to the location of the campsite where the rapist had been staying, and he had heard all of the details of his confession. The man had been hiding in the jungle just across the road from our school. He had been in that location for over a week, and during that time, he had been watching the other missionary and me on our morning walks. It had been his initial plan to take us as his victims, but "for some reason," he changed his mind at the very last minute.

I thank God for His promptings and for an attentive, praying mother! There is power in prayer, but I believe there is an added fervency when those prayers roll from the heart and lips of a mother and father for their child. The effectual fervent prayers of the righteous accomplish much. When those prayers are put into action and made effective by God, they are a powerful and dynamic force that stimulates change (see James 5:16 AMP).

The Deflection

Several years ago, I was privileged to be part of a missionary work team whose assignment was to build a home for a pastor and his family. It was an incredible project. It was actually supernatural! God enabled our small team to build that house from the concrete slab to a nearly completed home in just ten days. It was a hard, laborious task, but it was a joy to work with this amazing team and watch as this amazing project was being completed, one task at a time.

My friend and assistant, Darlene, was also on this trip, and while we are by no means professional carpenters, we were so honored to work alongside and assist those who were.

One part of the building that we were helping with was the framing of the inside walls of the home. With the use of power tools and pneumatic nail guns, the framing was going pretty quickly. Darlene was assisting one of the carpenters who was using the nail gun. She was holding the wall studs in place while he was nailing them.

As they worked on one wall, they were in a squatted position, and the carpenter using the nail gun was facing Darlene as she was holding the board being nailed. Somehow, the nail gun jerked just as he was pulling the trigger, and the nail missed the board and hit Darlene directly on her knee. Nail guns have a high-pressure force that can shoot a nail several feet and still penetrate the tip of the nail into a board. Darlene was right in front of the gun, just inches away, when the trigger was pulled. When the nail launched, hitting her knee, it was one of those moments when everything seemed to stand still as we were all left to watch helplessly as the event unfolded. It all happened so quickly, and there was absolutely no denying what should have happened. But God! The end result should have been a nail blasting into and causing severe damage to Darlene's knee, but instead, the end result was an amazing testimony of God's protection! Despite the tremendous pressure driving the nail forward, the Lord supernaturally caused it to simply tap and bounce off her knee and fall to the ground—not even leaving a mark on her!

It is so good and comforting to know that the watchful eye of Yahweh is upon us to provide His supernatural protection at just the right times. Even when we don't know it, He's working! He still works in ways we cannot see, His wonders to perform!

We join with the psalmist and declare, "The Lord is my strength and my shield; my heart trusted in Him, and I am helped; Therefore, my heart greatly rejoices, and with my song will I praise Him" (Psalm 28:7 NKJV).

15

The Impact of a Testimony

We are telling you about what we ourselves have actually seen and heard, so that you may share the fellowship and the joys we have with the Father and with Jesus Christ His Son.

–1 John 1:3 TLB

I have always loved reading in the gospels how Jesus called His disciples. Those common, ordinary people who were just going about their normal, everyday lives found their routines suddenly and abruptly halted as the Lord shifted them onto an entirely different course. Joy, excitement, fear, and uncertainty must have been part of the swirl of emotions they felt in those moments. They were not even completely sure, at first, that He was who He said He was, but still, something deep inside caused them to leave everything and follow Him. They chose to press beyond fear and uncertainty and take their place on the timeline of God's plan. They did their part for their time. They experienced God, and their experiences became testimonies that have impacted the generations, including our own. Those testimonies are not just fairytales; they are recorded accounts of true encounters and experiences with God, and they were "written for our learning."

In my late teen years, I began to realize that, like those disciples, our lives also have a part in God's plan that is ever unfolding. We are not called to replicate what others have already done, but we can learn from their testimonies and find inspiration and encouragement to take our own journey. What we glean from the stories of the generations that have gone before us gives us assurance that, wherever the Lord leads us, we can follow Him with a confident knowing that He is with us and that He is trustworthy and faithful to work through us.

The ninetieth Psalm was written by Moses. Now, there's a man with stories to tell! Within the words of this Psalm, Moses shared a profound revelation that he had received: "...We spend our years as a tale that is told" (Psalm 90:9 KJV). That revelation is true for us all. Every day that we live, our lives are telling our part of the story.

I wrote the following in my book, *Awakening the Church to Awaken a Nation*:

> The years of our lives are paragraphs and chapters written by our actions or our refusal to act, by our faith or our doubt, by our fear or our trust in God, our decisions, our conversations, our living, etc. It is all about writing a story for the next generation to read. Some are reading as we "write," and some

> will still "read" our stories long after we are gone. The great and sobering question is, what are we writing? What story are we leaving for the generations that are coming after us? Will our lives "write" the vision plain enough that those who read it may run with it?[1]

That's a sobering thought, and it's worth pondering.

Along my journey, I have encountered the Lord in many ways, and each time that I have seen Him work in my life, I have grown and matured in the knowledge of who He is and of who I am in Him. Through every step of faith, I have witnessed the truth of His Word being revealed in demonstration as He met me at each point of my obedience. I gave, and I received. I prayed in confident faith, and I witnessed His undeniable power to change unchangeable situations. I trusted my life into His care, and I experienced His protection. I haven't just heard *about* Him; I have *experienced* Him in many facets of who He is. Those experiences molded me, matured me, and persuaded me that He is always with me to work for me and through me both to will and to do His good pleasure.

One of the most valuable treasures that we have access to as born-again believers is the intellectual and experiential knowledge of God and of Jesus Christ that is ours for the receiving.

Experience is a powerful witness. It's not something that is based on speculation, supposition, or assumption; it is undeniable knowledge that is gained by direct observation. My best friend worked in surgery for many years. She said a common motto she often heard was, "See one. Do one. Teach one." Seeing impacts doing. Doing generates experience, and experience gives opportunity to teach others.

Intellectual knowledge is good, but when that knowledge is based on experience and not just mere words, it is powerful and compelling.

As I've lived my life and gathered my own experiences with the Lord, my great desire is now that I might be one who leaves deposits of the evidence of Christ's love and power that will provoke others to want to know Him.

May we all experience Him in His fullness. May we delve into all that God has provided, take Him at His Word, and find the valuable treasure of experience as we travel along our journey.

Like so many who have gone before us, may we be unashamed of God and of His power, and may we be unafraid of pure devotion that leads to undeniable testimonies that we can pass along to those around us. As John said, let's tell about the things that we ourselves have actually seen and heard so that others may share the fellowship and the joys that we have with the Father and with Jesus Christ His Son (see 1 John 1:3).

May our lives become so enriched with divine encounters that we become living epistles, declaring His mighty acts so that the goodness of God can continue to flow to a world that is groaning for evidence of Christ's love and of His reality.

16

Tell Your Stories

Be His witness to all men testifying of what you have seen and heard.

—Acts 22:15 AMP

As we read through the Old Testament, we find the recorded history of the nation of Israel. We see how God worked in supernatural and powerful ways to make Himself known to them and through them. We also discover that it was very important to God that the stories of their encounters with Him be told from generation to generation. In the book of Psalms, the writer reveals this truth, saying,

> Listen, O my people, to my teaching; incline your ears to the words of my mouth [and be willing to learn]. I will open my mouth in a parable [to instruct using examples]; I will utter dark and puzzling sayings of old [that contain important truth]—which we have heard and known, and our fathers have told us. We will not hide them from

> their children, but [we will] tell to the generation to come the praiseworthy deeds of the LORD, and [tell of] His great might and power and the wonderful works that He has done. For *He established a testimony* (a specific precept) in Jacob and appointed a law in Israel, which He commanded our fathers that they should teach to their children [the great facts of God's transactions with Israel], *that the generation to come might know them, that the children still to be born may arise and recount them to their children, that they should place their confidence in God and not forget the works of God,* but keep His commandments (Psalm 78:1-7 AMP).

These words give us great insight into the reason God wanted their stories to be told: so that generations to come would not forget His works. That compelling knowledge would then provoke them to believe that they could and should know and experience Him and His power for themselves.

Our experiences with God are stories that have been written on the pages of our lives, and those stories need to be told. Your stories matter. My stories matter. They matter to God, and they are needed by others. Regardless of how small or insignificant or how grand and amazing we may consider our stories to be, every experience with God is a treasure. They give us knowledge of who God is, and they have been written on our lives by the Author,

Himself, as He allowed us to see, feel, and experience the demonstration of His love, power, and reality. God has entrusted us with these experiences, and when shared, they have the ability to compel others to know that He is real and that His power is great and available to all who will believe.

As I was ministering one night, I said something to the effect that God is real and He is powerful. After the meeting, someone approached me and said, with tears flowing down her face, "When you made that statement that God is real and powerful, I leaned over to my husband and said, 'That's right! God *is* real! He *is* powerful!'" Then she uttered something to me that I thought was so profound. As I recall, she said, "I think sometimes we are so busy going through the routine motions of what we feel we are supposed to do–for example, praying, making decrees, doing prayer assignments, etc.–that we become focused on ourselves, and we unknowingly believe that the responsibility of the desired outcome is somehow based on our ability. But it's not! We are simply the vessel that God works through! He *is* real! He *is* powerful! We are the vessel, but it's His power that affects the outcome!"

As we avail ourselves to the Lord in obedience and devotion, He enables us to be vessels through which He makes His power known. As we experience His goodness and power in our own lives, He establishes a testimony in us that becomes a torch to light the way for others. Through those testimonies, the Lord preserves the sweetness of His goodness and power so that others will place their confidence in Him and not forget His works!

Our lives are a connection between what was and what is to come. We are His witnesses, and we must open our mouths and tell our stories. We must not keep our knowledge of the Lord to ourselves, holding our testimonies in our memories as though they are unimportant, undesirable, or unnecessary to be told. God, the great Author Himself, has written evidence of His reality on our lives, and to a world that is captive in gross darkness we must tell our stories so the light of His glory may shine to bring hope and deliverance and to light the way to lead them to Christ.

Take the Journey

As I have reflected back over the years of my life so far, I am amazed to see how God's hand has guided me. I see glimpses of just how involved He has been in orchestrating things and moments that have positioned me for His purposes, and I am overwhelmed by His love and ability! The people with whom He has connected me and how He connected us, places He has taken me, revelations He has given to me, opportunities He has led me into, disasters He helped me to avoid, situations and failures He's helped me to overcome, miracles, signs, and wonders He's allowed my eyes to behold–these are what I refer to as "fragrant moments." These are times when I knew that the Lord was really near to me and very involved and invested in my life. I see so many of these "fragrant moments" strewn throughout my journey so far, and my heart is overwhelmed with gratitude and wonder!

These experiences have helped to build a confident faith in me that has given me courage to stand and keep on standing. Life is not always easy. To walk by faith in God does not mean that we will never feel the weight of grief or be confronted with difficult times. There are challenges, obstacles, and uncertainties that we all go through. Although God may not be the Author of all these things, even in spite of these things, as we put our faith in Him, He will rise and reveal His ability to turn them for our good and for His glory. In the most desperate and difficult times of life, when it seemed that there was no hope for change, I have witnessed God's power working on my behalf, and those moments have left me with an unshakeable awareness of and confidence in Him.

With our faith and focus on the Lord, we may go through trials, but we will emerge with triumph and with experience that proves His reality and steadfast faithfulness. That's not to say that everything will always work out the way we think it should, but we can always trust that God is with us and that He always knows what is best. The more we experience the reality of Jesus and the undeniable power of God working in and through our lives, the more we grow and are secured in our faith in Him. Jesus becomes more than a historic figure from long ago; He is our victorious, reigning King! God becomes more than a Bible character; He is our real and present Father, Friend, Help, and Guide.

Before us is a journey that is filled with adventure, potential, and purpose. For the young and for the old, that journey is ours for the taking. A relationship with God through the acceptance of Jesus as Lord and Savior of our lives is the starting block that launches us into the discovery of the destinies for which we were created. The plan is there, but the path must be chosen. If we choose the path, His promise is that He will lead us and equip us with all that we need to fulfill our part in His plan.

This journey of faith that I have chosen is not something that I choose because of mere words that I have heard or read. I take this journey with confidence because of what I have seen with my own eyes and experienced in my own life and have witnessed in the lives of others. This book is a collection of just a few of those experiences. In the previous pages, you have read only some of God's provision, guidance, supernatural intervention, miracles, signs, and wonders that I have witnessed. I pray that the words you have read have painted a clear and undeniable picture of the reality of the power, love, and guidance that the Lord avails to all who are saved and willing to give Him their devotion.

God's power is not exclusive to a select few. We each, as born-again believers, have access to all that God is and to all that He makes available to us through Jesus and through faith in His name. I only share my personal experiences to serve as examples of how God leads us and works for us and through us...and that God *does* lead us and work for and through us. I am nothing great. *God* is great! He is holy, and He is approachable. He invites us to come boldly into His presence and to make our petitions known to Him. He loves to work on our behalf, and His work in us and through us actually reveals Him to others. He has entrusted us with these experiences, and to share them is to share the reality of Him and to bring recognition and honor to Him.

It is my hope and prayer that my stories will build your faith and inspire you to tell your own stories, so that others can know the joy of trusting and following God.

If you don't know Jesus Christ as your Savior, it is my ultimate prayer that my stories will reveal Him to you and compel you to desire to know Him for yourself. He has purpose and destiny for your life, too, and they are found in a relationship with Him. Your stories are just waiting to be discovered and told.

For my fellow sojourners who are on the path, experiencing God's power and presence, I pray this book will inspire you to keep traveling and to continue to tell your stories. As God, through Ananias, instructed Paul, so He instructs us to be a witness to all men of what we have seen and heard (see Acts 22:15).

For those who may read this book who have been deterred by perceived obstacles or fears, I pray these stories will encourage you to take those leaps of faith that will allow you to venture out beyond the place of comfort and familiarity! It's not too late. It's time! Whether God leads you into business or career ventures, ministry opportunities, or prayer assignments for your family, region, or nations—wherever His path may lead you—take the journey. The Lord has great things to reveal to you and through you! Your obedience to follow His path will enable you to experience God in amazing ways, and those experiences will create testimonies that will empower you with an even greater ability to be a living witness for Christ.

The journey awaits us all. It is ever unfolding, and the Lord's beckoning call to each of us is, "Come, follow Me." Don't allow the fog of uncertainty to deter you. Follow the Guide, and discover all of the amazing adventures, encounters, and divine opportunities that God has placed on your path.

The knowing is in the going, so go! Experience Him, and then tell your stories so that others may know that He is real and that the journey is so worth taking!

Notes

Chapter 1 The Knowing is in the Going

1. John A. Shedd, *Salt from My Attic*, (Portland: Mosher Press,1928)

2. Kay Arthur, *As Silver Refined: Learning to Embrace Life's Disappointments*, (Colorado Springs: WaterBrook Press, 1999)

Chapter 3 Have Faith in God

1. James Strong, *Strong's Exhaustive Concordance of the Bible* (McLean, Va.: MacDonald Publishing, 1990), Greek 996

Chapter 4 Persuaded Faith

1. F. F. Bosworth, *Christ the Healer*, 9th ed. (Grand Rapids: Fleming H. Revell, 1973, 2000) 84

Chapter 7 I've Known Him As Healer

1. James Strong, *Strong's Exhaustive Concordance of the Bible* (McLean, Va.: MacDonald Publishing, 1990), Greek 7495

2. Kenneth Copeland Ministries, "4 Testimonies of God's Manifest Power through the Ministry of Angels, Testimony No. 1: Supernatural Surgery through Angels," KCM blog, February 13, 2020, https://blog.kcm.org/4-testimonies-of-gods-manifest-power-through-the-ministry-of-angels/.

3. Gina Gholston, "The Mantle of Revival" & "Carry on with the Mantle," in *Carry On: Becoming Faithful Stewards of*

Our Spiritual Inheritance, ed. Jim Bryson (Sharpsburg, Md.: Spring Mill Publishing LLC, 2023), 36-46

Chapter 12 A Time of Launching

1. Gina Gholston, “America Shall be Saved,” in *Awakening the Church to Awaken a Nation: Finding Wisdom and Strategies for Our Times through Prophetic Dreams, Visions, and Revelation,* ed. Jim Bryson (Sharpsburg, Md.: Spring Mill Publishing LLC, 2020), 77-78

2. Gholston, “For an Appointed Time” & “The Turning Point,” in *Awakening the Church to Awaken a Nation,* 37-41, 51-52

Chapter 15 The Impact of a Testimony

1. Gina Gholston, “The Point of Connection,” in *Awakening the Church to Awaken a Nation: Finding God’s Wisdom and Strategies for Our Times through Prophetic Dreams, Visions, and Revelation,* ed. Jim Bryson (Sharpsburg, Md.: Spring Mill Publishing LLC 2020), 72-73

About the Author

Gina Gholston entered a personal relationship with the Lord Jesus Christ at a young age. Fully surrendering her life to the Lord, she was launched into a journey toward fulfilling her God-given purposes.

Having briefly lived as a missionary and having also traveled with the organization called Men and Women of Action (based in Cleveland, TN) to many nations, Gina has assisted in various humanitarian and disaster relief mission efforts for the purpose of bringing the hope and love of Christ to some of the most remote places of the world.

Gina has served in ministry for over forty-one years now. She is a prophetic minister—a revivalist at heart—who ministers under the anointing and power of the Holy Spirit. Through preaching, prayer, and prophetic declaration, she contends for an awakening to an awareness of God that will lead to revival and reformation in the Church and in the nation. Her desire is to always honor and bring glory to God and to His Son, Jesus Christ. A prophetic dreamer, Gina's dreams and visions have been, and are being, used as strategy for prayer, prayer assignments, and insight to assist the Church in taking Her place to bring an awakening to God in America. Many have given voice to her dreams, visions, and prophetic words in conferences and ministry platforms by sharing them in their messages, books, social media posts, and podcasts.

A best-selling author, Gina has filled her three previous books—*Awakening the Church to Awaken a Nation*, *Dreams of Awakening*, and *Carry On*—with prophetic dreams, visions, and prophetic words with which the Lord has entrusted her. Also included are many biblical teachings and personal experiences.

Gina is a native and lifetime resident of the beautiful state of Tennessee.

More from Gina Gholston

Awakening the Church to Awaken a Nation

In *Awakening the Church to Awaken a Nation*, Gina Gholston shares prophetic dreams, visions, and prophetic insights that have been given to her by God for the purpose of revealing wisdom and strategy concerning His intentions for our time and for our nation. The words of this book will challenge you to know your identity in Christ and to listen above the chaos to hear God's Kingdom strategies that are being poured out by Holy Spirit in our times.

Dreams of Awakening

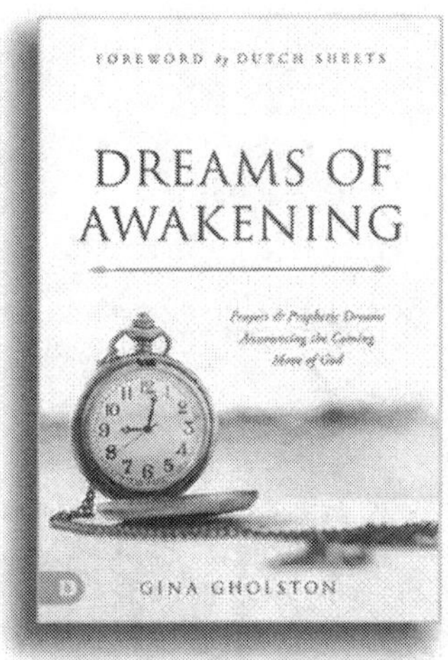

In *Dreams of Awakening*, Gina Gholston presents detailed dreams and visions she has received from the Lord, along with their interpretations. Each of the prophetic revelations highlights a resounding call for the Body of Christ to rise and shine as lights in darkness. Each chapter features a powerful prophetic dream and corresponding prayer activation, helping you wage warfare prayer to bring about His promises of awakening.

Carry On

In *Carry On*, Gina Gholston shares dreams, visions, prophetic words, and scriptural insights that help to uncover the truth and content of our spiritual inheritance that was demonstrated in the life of Jesus and in the lives of those within the early Church. God has given to us an amazing inheritance, and it manifests in and through us by the power and supervision of the Holy Ghost. As you read through the pages of this book, you will be inspired and provoked to receive, experience, and to carry on with the fullness of all that belongs to you as a child of God.

To order Gina's books, you may visit her website:

www.ginagholston.com

You may also order Gina's books via Amazon.com.

Contact Info

Mailing Address:

Gina Gholston

P.O. Box 30781

Clarksville, TN 37040

Email:

ggministries20@gmail.com

Website:

www.ginagholston.com

Facebook:

www.facebook.com/ginagholstonministries/

Truth Social:

ginagholston@ginagholston

YouTube Channel:

Gina Gholston Ministries

Made in the USA
Columbia, SC
09 June 2025